Garde FOR DUMMIES
PORTABLE EDITION

by Michael MacCaskey
with Bill Marken
& the Editors of The National
Gardening Association

WILEY

Wiley Publishing, Inc.

Gardening For Dummies®, Portable Edition

Published by
Wiley Publishing, Inc.
111 River St.
Hoboken, NJ 07030-5774
www.wiley.com

For general information on our other products and services, please contact our Customer Care Department within the U.S. at 800-762-2974, outside the U.S. at 317-572-3993, or fax 317-572-4002.

For technical support, please visit www.wiley.com/techsupport.

Wiley also publishes its books in a variety of electronic formats. Some content that appears in print may not be available in electronic books.

Library of Congress Control Number: 2006922232

ISBN-13: 978-0-470-04465-0

ISBN-10: 0-470-04465-9

Manufactured in the United States of America

10 9 8 7 6 5 4 3 2 1

1B/QR/QT/QW/IN

WILEY

About the Authors

Michael MacCaskey: Michael MacCaskey began his college career as a creative arts student at San Francisco State University in 1969, but in the process became instead a passionate gardener. By 1976, he received a Bachelor of Science degree in ornamental horticulture from California State Polytechnic University, San Luis Obispo. Since then, he's had the good fortune to work for and learn from garden editors such as Walter Doty, Richard Dunmire, Joe Williamson, and Bill Marken. A second-generation Los Angeles native (zone 9), he was appointed editor-in-chief of Vermont-based *National Gardening* magazine (zone 4) in 1994. Since then, he's been learning about gardening in a short-season, cold-winter region. His magazine writing has been honored by both the Western Magazine Publishers Association and the Garden Writers of America.

Bill Marken: Bill Marken is the editor of *Rebecca's Garden Magazine,* a publication from Hearst Magazine Enterprises based on the popular television show. A lifelong resident of California, Bill served as editor-in-chief of *Sunset,* the Magazine of Western Living, from 1981 to 1996. Earlier in his career, he wrote for the magazine's garden section, pitched in on several editions of the best-selling *Western Garden Book,* and generally nurtured his interests in subjects related to gardening, landscaping, travel, and other aspects of the good life in the West. A vacation garden at 6,200-feet elevation gives him insight into cold-winter climates with 100-day growing seasons.

National Gardening Association: The National Gardening Association is the largest member-based, nonprofit organization of home gardeners in the U.S. It was founded in 1972 (as "Gardens for All") to spearhead the community garden movement. For more information about the National Gardening Association, write to 180 Flynn Ave., Burlington, VT 05401; or check out its Web site at www.garden.org.

Publisher's Acknowledgments

We're proud of this book; please send us your comments through our Dummies online registration form located at www.dummies.com/register/.

Some of the people who helped bring this book to market include the following:

Acquisitions, Editorial, and Media Development

Project Editor: Elizabeth Kuball

Editorial Program Coordinator: Hanna K. Scott

Editorial Manager: Michelle Hacker

Editorial Assistants: Erin Calligan, David Lutton

Cover Photos: © Ingram Publishing

Cartoons: Rich Tennant (www.the5thwave.com)

Composition Services

Project Coordinator: Kristie Rees

Layout and Graphics: Carl Byers, Andrea Dahl, Joyce Haughey, Brent Savage

Special Art: Ron Hildebrand, Hildebrand Design

Proofreaders: Joe Niesen

Indexer: Sherry Massey

Special Help

Carmen Krikorian, Katie Foote

Publishing and Editorial for Consumer Dummies

Diane Graves Steele, Vice President and Publisher, Consumer Dummies

Joyce Pepple, Acquisitions Director, Consumer Dummies

Kristin A. Cocks, Product Development Director, Consumer Dummies

Michael Spring, Vice President and Publisher, Travel

Kelly Regan, Editorial Director, Travel

Publishing for Technology Dummies

Andy Cummings, Vice President and Publisher, Dummies Technology/General User

Composition Services

Gerry Fahey, Vice President of Production Services

Debbie Stailey, Director of Composition Services

Contents at a Glance

Introduction...**1**

Chapter 1: Just a Few Ground-Level Questions and Answers 5

Chapter 2: Zoning Out: What You Can and Can't Grow 13

Chapter 3: Tools of the Trade 29

Chapter 4: Understanding and Improving Soil 43

Chapter 5: Choosing and Planting Seedlings, Trees, and Shrubs.......63

Chapter 6: Growing Food Gardens 79

Chapter 7: Feed Me, Seymour! Watering, Feeding, and
Composting...101

Chapter 8: Fighting Pests and Diseases...............................125

Chapter 9: Winning the War against Weeds 153

Chapter 10: Ten (Or So) Tips for Gardening in Tight Spaces............159

Index...**165**

Table of Contents

Introduction *1*

About the Authors 3
About This Book 1
Conventions Used in This Book 2
What You're Not to Read...................................2
Foolish Assumptions 2
Icons Used in This Book.....................................3
Where to Go from Here 4

Chapter 1: Just a Few Ground-Level Questions and Answers 5

How Do I Make My Plants Grow Rather Than Die? 6
Your climate and microclimates 6
Sun or shade...7
Soil and water...8
Plants that are most at home in your garden 8
What Can I Use My Garden For?............................9
Do I Have to Learn a Foreign Language? 10
The fancy name...11
Common names 12

Chapter 2: Zoning Out: What You Can and Can't Grow 13

Plant Hardiness 14
The USDA Plant Hardiness Zone Map 15
The chill factor..15
USDA zone shortcomings 16
The American Horticultural Society's Plant Heat-Zone Map...16
Length Counts: How Long Is Your Season?.................18
Stretching Your Garden Season.............................19
Planting earlier in the year 20
Gardening beyond autumn.............................23
Gardening all year..24
Maximizing Winter Hardiness 25

Chapter 3: Tools of the Trade 29

Hand Tools 29
The magnificent seven tools 30
Hand-tool maintenance 32
Five more tools to buy 32
Powering Up Your Tools 34
Lawn mowers 34
Trimmers 37
Tillers and grinders 38
Where to Shop for Garden Tools 41
Nurseries 42
Other sources for tools and garden supplies 42

Chapter 4: Understanding and Improving Soil 43

Clearing the Site 43
Stripping sod 44
Other soil-clearing methods 45
Meeting Your Soil 46
Soil texture 47
Soil structure 49
One more big thing: Soil pH 51
Your soil, in detail 52
Improving Your Soil 52
Exactly what do you add? 54
Changing pH 56
Adding nutrients 57
Green manure crops and cover crops 57
Loosening the Soil 58
Time for a tiller 59
Double digging 60
Simple raised beds 61

Chapter 5: Choosing and Planting Seedlings, Trees, and Shrubs 63

Buying and Planting Seedlings 64
Figuring Out Spacing for Transplants 65
Planting Seedlings, Step by Step 65
Container-Grown Trees and Shrubs 68
Choosing container-grown trees and shrubs 69
Transplanting trees and shrubs from containers 70
Bare-Root Planting 74
Choosing bare-root plants 74
Planting bare-root plants 74

Burlap-Wrapped Root Balls 75
    Choosing balled-and-burlapped plants.....................75
    Planting balled-and-burlapped plants.......................76

Chapter 6: Growing Food Gardens. 79

Planning a Vegetable Garden....................................79
    Seasonal preferences 80
    Choose the right location 81
    Make the garden the right size.............................82
    Designing the garden...83
    Improving the soil..84
    What to start with..85
    It's all in the timing 85
    Raise them right..86
    Have a happy harvest 87
You Can't Go Wrong with These..............................88
What about Hybrids and Heirlooms? 89
Squeezing in Herbs 90
Is There Fruit in Your Future?.................................92
    Six steps to a fruit-tree harvest...........................93
    Planning a fruit garden..95
    Fruits for the home garden..................................95

**Chapter 7: Feed Me, Seymour! Watering,
Feeding, and Composting 101**

Watering Basics 102
    Getting water to your garden 103
    Determining the amount and frequency of
        watering 106
    Conserving water...108
Providing a Balanced Diet for Your Plants.............109
Don't Compromise, Fertilize!..................................111
    Common fertilizer terms......................................111
    Kinds of fertilizers for various plants 114
    Organic fertilizers 115
Piling Onto the Compost Bandwagon 116
    From refuse to riches 117
    Bin there, done that!...118
    To build or to buy? 118
    Composting aids . . . who needs them?.................121
    Heapin' it on 122

Chapter 8: Fighting Pests and Diseases 125

Insect Pests You're Most Likely to Encounter......................126
    Aphids 126
    Apple maggots 126
    Bean leaf beetles..127
    Black vine weevils..127
    Borers..127
    Caterpillars 128
    Chinch bugs..128
    Codling moths 128
    Colorado potato beetles 129
    Corn earworms 129
    Cucumber beetles...129
    Curculios...130
    Cutworms 130
    Flea beetles..131
    Gypsy moths 131
    Japanese beetles...131
    Leaf miners 133
    Mealybugs...133
    Mexican bean beetles.......................................133
    Oriental fruit moths..133
    Root maggots 134
    Scale 134
    Snails and slugs..134
    Spider mites..135
    Tarnished plant bugs (lygus bugs)....................136
    Tent caterpillars...136
    Tomato hornworms...136
    Whiteflies 137
Managing Pests 137
    Encouraging "good" insects 138
    Safe and effective pest chemicals....................139
Preventing Plant Diseases...145
    Solarization...145
    More than a dozen dirty diseases: What to do........146
    Least-toxic disease remedies 150

Chapter 9: Winning the War against Weeds 153

Weed-Control Basics...153
Nontoxic Herbicides..155
Common Weeds...155
    Bindweed (Convolvulus arvensis) 155
    Bermuda grass (Cynodon dactylon)...................156

Chickweed (Stellaria media) 156
Crabgrass (Digitaria)...156
Curly dock (Rumex crispus) 157
Dandelion (Taraxacum officinale) 157
Lamb's-quarters (Chenopodium album) 157
Oxalis...157
Purslane (Portulaca oleracea) 158
Redroot pigweed (Amaranthus retroflexus) 158
Shepherd's purse (Capsella bursa-pastoris).............158
Spotted (or prostrate) spurge....................................158

**Chapter 10: Ten (Or So) Tips for Gardening
in Tight Spaces 159**

Keep It Simple..159
Pay Attention to the Details.......................................160
Vary Levels..161
Try Some Visual Trickery 161
Borrow a View 162
Plant in Gaps...162
Cover Up with Climbers..162
Plant Overhead...162
Be Choosey about What You Include in Your Garden........163

Index *165*

Introduction

*T*hink about how people once talked about gardens and gardening. For most folks, those terms usually meant a rectangular patch of ground — somewhere out back — where they grew a few vegetables or flowers. Gardens were practical, plain, and utilitarian.

But now, the word *gardening* signifies so much more. Gardening is all about a process that delights the eye and fuels the soul with a connection to the Earth. Gardening is good for the body. An hour or two of weeding, harvesting, or cultivating provides just the right kind of light exercise we all need. Responsible gardening also does good things for the environment: Materials get recycled and empty lots become community gardens, for example.

Gardening now encompasses our lives — if you have a yard, even a very tiny one, you are a gardener. If you have a sunny windowsill, you are a gardener. National surveys show that gardening has become the most popular, least exclusive hobby of all. Everybody is doing it.

About This Book

You have in your hands a gardening encyclopedia in miniature — all you need to know to get off to a good start. In every chapter, our basic goal is to give you the information you need to go out and grow what you want.

This book is a reference book, which means you can flip to the pages that you need now — you don't have to read the entire book from beginning to end in one sitting, although you're welcome to if you want!

Conventions Used in This Book

In this book, we use a few conventions, explained here:

- Whenever we define a new term, we put the term in *italics,* with the definition close at hand.

- Any Web addresses or e-mail address appear in `monofont`, so you know where the address starts and stops.

- Plant names are made up of the genus, species, variety, and sometime the cultivar. All this is explained in depth in Chapter 1, but what you need to know here is that you'll often seen plant names in italics and portions of the names with single quotes. If you want the skinny on which part of name is which, turn to Chapter 1.

For international gardeners, we've added approximate metric equivalents for plant heights, planting depths, and other pertinent measurements.

What You're Not to Read

Because this book is a reference, you don't need to read everything between the covers. You can skip sidebars (text in gray boxes) without missing the key points of the chapter — but if you have the time and the inclination, you'll find some interesting and useful information there.

Foolish Assumptions

We don't make many assumptions about our readers, but we do assume that you're interested in gardening of some sort — whether you want to grow fruits and vegetables, a field of flowers, or just a small container on your doorstep. We don't assume you have any background in gardening — and we definitely don't assume that you have a green thumb! Green thumb or not, this book can help you achieve your gardening goals.

But novices aren't the only ones who will find this book useful. Gardening is such a huge topic that no one ever comes close to knowing everything about it. (That's one reason why gardening has become one of the most popular hobbies of all time.)

Icons Used in This Book

Icons are those little pictures in the margin that direct your attention to key pieces of information. Here's what they mean:

 Suggests ways to save money.

 Points out ecological tips and ways to be earth-friendly.

 Flags information that even some experienced gardeners may not know.

 Marks tips that experienced gardeners live by.

 Offers international gardening advice and data.

Demystifies gardening lingo. Although we've made this book as jargon-free as possible, you need to know some terms.

Gives addresses and/or phone numbers for ordering special gardening equipment.

Watch out! Alerts you to avoid bad gardening experiences, including some that may cause injury.

Where to Go from Here

You've got your copy of *Gardening For Dummies,* Portable Edition — now what? Get answers to common questions in Chapter 1; discover your zone in Chapter 2; or discover everything you need to know about watering, feeding, and composting in Chapter 7. Or start at the beginning and read straight through to the end!

Chapter 1

Just a Few Ground-Level Questions and Answers

. . . .

In This Chapter

▶ Understanding what plants need from you

▶ Knowing what your garden can do for you

▶ Speaking the garden language

. . . .

*I*f you want to find out more about gardening — and you must if you're reading this — just where do you start? We could start with some heavy-duty science, tossing around terms like *cotyledon, cambium,* and the ever-popular *pith.* Or we could start talking about beautiful gardens like critics of fine paintings — employing words like *composition, energy, focal point,* and such.

We don't mean to suggest anything but respect for scientists and artists. In fact, the chance to combine science and art is what draws many of us to gardening in the first place — especially if you throw in a little farming and a few old wives' tales (of course, you should or shouldn't plant sweet peas at the full moon).

All we really want to do here is get you through a few basic principles of plant growth and garden planning so that you can rush out into the yard when the weather's right for planting and the soil is ripe for digging.

First, any questions?

How Do I Make My Plants Grow Rather Than Die?

Like other living things, plants have certain requirements for good health. For example, they require the right amounts of sunlight, moisture, and nutrients. Plants also need an equitable range of temperatures — neither too hot nor too cold.

When selecting plants, you can meet their requirements in one of two ways. The first involves selecting your favorite plants and then doing your best to alter the growing conditions at the planting site to meet their needs. You can change the growing conditions by adding sprinkler irrigation, incorporating fertilizer, hauling in fresh topsoil, pruning some trees, or covering plants with blankets in winter. But this is the backward approach.

A better way to make sure plants grow well — and need less care in the process — is to find out the conditions at the planting site first and then choose plants that grow under those conditions. Of course, some of the plants that you want to put in are accustomed to conditions different from what you have in your yard, and those plants are going to need some attention to stay happy. But the better you match plants to the planting site, the longer the plants will live, the better the plants will look, and the less work (watering, pruning, fertilizing, and controlling pests) you'll have to do to care for them.

Your climate and microclimates

Matching a plant to a planting site needs to be done on both a large and a small scale. On a large scale, a plant needs to be adapted to the general climate of the area in which it lives. Can the plant withstand winter's low temperatures and summer's high temperatures? Is the annual rainfall enough to keep the plant alive, or will it need supplemental irrigation? Understanding your climate is a huge step toward successful gardening — Chapter 2, in fact, is devoted to climates.

On a smaller scale, can the plant grow well in the localized climate of your yard or the planting site? Smaller climates, called *microclimates,* can be quite a bit different from the overall climate of your area. For example, because of the shadows that your house casts, the northern side of your house is cooler and shadier than its southern side. Or a planting site located beside a white, west-facing wall can be several degrees warmer than the rest of the yard because of the reflected heat from the wall.

Sun or shade

All plants need light to grow properly. However, the amount of light that plants need varies.

Many plants require full sun for at least six to eight hours per day. Plants that don't get enough sunlight become *leggy* (with long, spindly stems), as if stretching out for more light. Plants that don't get enough sunlight also tend to flower poorly.

Some plants prefer shady conditions for the entire day (or for at least part of the day). Many different types of shade exist, and each type of shade creates a different microclimate. For example, consider the area on the east side of your house. For at least half a day — in the morning — this area is sunny and warm. In the afternoon, the same area is shady.

The west side of the house is usually just the opposite — shady in the morning but hot and sunny in the afternoon. Heavy, all-day shade appears on the north side of the house, and filtered shade is found under trees. To further confuse the matter, shade can change with the seasons as trees lose their leaves and as the sun moves on the horizon. And in the hottest climates, some normally sun-loving plants prefer at least partial afternoon shade.

Note one obvious rule for gardening in the shade: Put shade-loving plants in the shade. Sun-worshipping plants just won't make it. Don't fret. Hundreds of incredible shade-loving plants (some with showy flowers and others with attractive foliage and form) are available to choose from.

To make matters just a little complicated, a plant's shade tolerance varies both by region and by specific garden conditions. For example, many plants that need full sun in cool northern climates (or in coastal areas) tolerate or require some afternoon shade when grown in warm southern climates.

Soil and water

The kind of soil in your garden — heavy clay or porous sand, for example — and soil moisture are closely related. Chapters 4 and 7 detail the importance of these two factors and the ways in which they affect plant growth. Those chapters also cover cultural practices such as tilling, watering, and fertilizing. Whether you see desert, snow, or palm trees when you look out your window, you can find plants that are well adapted to almost every situation. Wet, soggy clay soil is very difficult to correct, but certain plants can grow, and even thrive, under those conditions. Choosing plants to fit existing soil conditions is usually a great deal easier than altering the soil conditions themselves.

Plants that are most at home in your garden

Nothing epitomizes the principle of choosing plants appropriate to the site more than growing *native plants*. Natives are plants that grow naturally in a specific region or locality. Over hundreds (probably thousands) of years, these plants have become superbly adapted to the exact conditions of the areas to which they are native. In those areas or in similar areas, native plants grow with health and vigor and without the help of gardeners — abilities that make them very valuable as landscape plants.

Native plants are becoming very popular in many areas, particularly in arid regions of the western United States. Thirsty, nonnative plants are impractical in these areas because they use too much of a precious resource — water. Local native plants can get by on what nature provides. And conserving natural resources always makes sense.

Using native plants also helps the native fauna — the birds, butterflies, squirrels, and other local animals — that depend on native plants for food and shelter.

Many retail nurseries can help you select native plants. Some mail-order catalogs also specialize in native plants, especially wildflowers.

What Can I Use My Garden For?

True, you can go buy plants and stick them in the ground —
and let it go at that. But many of us want a *garden,* which, by
our definition, contains enough organization and space to
allow room for growing plants plus other purposes — playing,
relaxing, outdoor dining, entertaining, and more.

A garden can make your life more comfortable, healthier,
more colorful, and more convenient. A garden lets you expand
your living area to the outdoors, harvest fresh food, and pick
your own flowers. Take a look at the different ways that a
garden can enhance your life:

- **A garden can be a private getaway.** Imagine taking a
  vacation in your own backyard or relaxing in a shady
  spot, secluded from the hustle and bustle of daily living.
  This dream can be yours, if you begin by creating a private area for your own pleasure.

- **A garden can be a place for entertaining.** Whether you
  like large get-togethers with the extended family or business associates or a quiet dinner with a few friends, your
  garden can provide an ideal atmosphere. You need a few
  key ingredients to make your garden perfect for entertaining.

- **A garden can be a place for children and pets.** Who will
  use your garden? Take into account kids and pets — they
  have different garden interests than grownups.

- **A garden can be your very own flower shop.** Cutting an
  armful of flowers from your own garden and bringing
  them indoors is so satisfying. If you like freshly cut flowers, be sure to leave space to grow your own.

- **A garden can be a source of food.** One of the most delicious aspects of your garden is that it can produce wonderful vegetables, fruits, and herbs. You can grow
  gourmet produce, rare and special crops — and you can
  grow them organically.

- **A garden can be a practical work area.** Being outdoors
  means more than fun and games. You may need a place
  in your yard to keep your garden tools, heating fuel tank,
  firewood, clothesline, or garbage cans. Organize all these
  less-than-attractive outdoor necessities into the same

out-of-the way location — a workstation separate from your entertaining and play areas. Ideally, the location should be handy, near the garage or driveway, but far enough away from handsome views or gardens so that the workstation is not a distraction.

✔ **A garden can be a place to relax.** Anywhere that seems cozy and pleasant is a great place to put a sitting nook. The area doesn't have to be fancy, just a place for you to relax and, perhaps, watch the kids play. Start with a comfortable bench or chair and position it in shade beneath a magnificent oak, at the end of your vegetable garden, or at the back of your yard near the swing set. If you put in all-weather footing — gravel or mulch, for example — you can sit outside regardless of the soil conditions.

The possibilities for your garden are almost endless. Take some time to jot down everything you may want in your yard.

Do I Have to Learn a Foreign Language?

The language spoken in gardening circles can be quirky. For example, dirt isn't just *dirt*, it's *soil*. Dirt is what you make mud pies with; it's the stain on your shirt. Soil, on the other hand, is full of promise and good nutrients. And some gardenholics tend to go on and on about plant names. You may catch them at the nursery asking, "Which Latin name is *most* correct: the old one or the new one?" or "What is the proper pronunciation for that plant?" Real garden snobs even get into heated debates about how to spell a particular plant name. Don't be too hard on these people. Not only can they not help themselves, but you may find yourself behaving the same way someday.

In other words, learning something about plant names helps you appreciate gardening more — and helps you get through this book.

The fancy name

The proper (scientific) *botanical name* of a plant consists of two parts, much in the same way that people have a first and a last name. However, in plant language, the last name comes first.

The most important name is the *genus* — the "Smith" of Joe Smith, if you will. (The genus name always begins with a capital letter when used as part of a multipart name.) A genus is a group of closely related plants. Just as in your own family, some of the plant cousins look a lot alike, while others don't bear much resemblance at all. Also like your family, some closely related individuals have very different comfort levels. One uncle lives in Phoenix, Arizona, and loves the heat. His sister thinks that Oxford, England, is quite warm enough, thank you very much. It's the same for plants.

The second name, the "Joe" part of Joe Smith, is the *species* name. The species name usually describes some feature of the plant or its preferred habitat, or serves as a tribute to whoever discovered the plant. But the species name is disguised in pseudo-Latin, of course, just to keep things interesting. Consider, for example, *Hosta undulata. Hosta* is the genus name. The species name, *undulata,* describes the undulating shape of the leaf.

The plain, old-fashioned, natural species of some plants acquire new status in the face of prodigiously hybridized plants — tulips, for example. In those cases, the norm for the plant is some kind of hybrid of indeterminate botanical origin. That's why, when gardeners finally have in their gardens an actual natural, nonhybridized type of tulip, they say something like, "And this is my species tulip." Gardeners are funny, aren't they? (In this book, we use the abbreviation *sp.* for *species.*)

Occasionally, a third name follows the species name — the variety. *Varieties* are members of the same species but are different enough to deserve their own name. Just as you may have one redhead in a family of brunettes, some plants are quite dissimilar to their siblings. For example, *Lychnis coronaria* bears magenta flowers. Her sister *Lychnis coronaria alba,* however, wears a white *(alba)* flower.

Another part of a botanical name is the cultivated variety, or *cultivar.* Whoever discovered or created the plant decided that it was special enough to have its own name. And the cultivar is also special enough to be maintained by cuttings, grafting, line-bred seed propagation, or tissue culture. The cultivar name appears after the species or variety name. The cultivar name is the only part of the botanical name that isn't in italics but is always enclosed with single quotation marks. For example, a very nice form of *Lychnis coronaria* with a pink blush is called *Lychnis coronaria* 'Angel Blush.'

Common names

Of course, ordinary people don't go around using long Latin botanical names in everyday conversation. Instead, they use a sort of botanical nickname, called a *common name.* Common names are less formal and easier to pronounce than botanical names. They're also less precise. Just as your Aunt Norma calls you "pumpkin" and Uncle Bob calls you "big guy," many plants have several nicknames.

Often, the common name describes some distinguishing characteristic of the plant. For example, the plant called "blue star" has starry blue flowers. Sometimes, the origin of the name is lost in the mythology of a former time. Does anyone have a clue just who was the Susan of black-eyed Susan fame?

Finding that several unrelated flowers share the same common name isn't unusual at all. Unfortunately, regular English flower names are often just as silly as their highfalutin Latin cousins, if for different reasons. For example, two distinct plants share the name "mock orange," and at least five different plants go by "dusty miller." At least three unrelated perennials are called "coneflowers": *Echinacea purpurea,* the *Rudbeckia* genus, and the *Ratibida* genus. On the other hand, many plants have no common name! Go figure.

The long and short of it is that you need to pay some attention to plant names — if only to avoid buying and planting the wrong plant.

Chapter 2

Zoning Out: What You Can and Can't Grow

● ●

In This Chapter

▶ Understanding which permanent plants can grow in your garden

▶ Looking at USDA zones for plants' winter hardiness

▶ Getting to know the Sunset system

▶ Finding out about heat zones

▶ Creating frost-free days for annuals and vegetables

▶ Extending the growing season

▶ Maximizing winter hardiness

● ●

*E*ver hear the gardener's favorite pickup line? It's "Hi, what's your zone?" If the response is neither stony silence nor a slap across the face, you're in luck — you've met another gardener. Now if someone has asked you this question and you had no idea how to respond, this chapter is for you. But this chapter is also useful for anyone trying to decide which permanent plants — trees, shrubs, ground covers, herbaceous perennials, and vines — to choose based on plant hardiness.

Why do you need to worry about zones with only permanent plants? These plants need to survive weather conditions that vary year-round in your garden: cool, wet weather; extreme heat or cold; and drought, for example. Year-round conditions are not an issue for most vegetables and similar annuals; these plants don't start growing until spring, and then they die in fall. What's important for annuals and vegetables is the *length* of that growing season, the number of days between frosts. (You read more about frost-free days later in this chapter.)

Plant Hardiness

Gardeners are keenly aware of the seasonal effects of temperature, particularly freezing temperatures, on the growth of landscape plants. Terms such as *cold hardy, frost hardy,* and *winter hardy* describe plants that can survive varying degrees of freezing temperatures without injury during winter dormancy.

Some very large and substantial plants curl their toes and turn mushy if exposed long enough to low temperatures. Imagine a banana tree thriving all summer in Duluth, Minnesota, and then imagine what happens to it in September. On the other hand, some plants can survive freezing, and even frigid, temperatures. Some escape the cold by hiding underground or under snow until spring. These plants include the bulbs and many perennials. Others, such as hardy trees and shrubs, undergo metabolic changes between summer and winter.

The genetic capacity of a plant to acclimate determines cold hardiness. When plants acclimate, they transform themselves from a nonhardy to hardy condition that allows them to withstand freezing temperatures. But absolute temperature, as devastating as its effects can be, is not the only criterion of hardiness. Many plants are injured not in winter by minimum temperatures, but in spring and fall as they adjust to changing weather. At those times, while not growing at full tilt, plants are not fully hardy either. So you can see that determining where and when a plant is hardy can be complicated. Temperatures are crucial, but so are a region's climate patterns and how the plant responds.

Winter injury is easy to diagnose when you see lots of brown leaves on an evergreen plant, injury or death of flower buds, or splitting bark. But sometimes damage from winter temperatures is difficult to see, manifested only in delayed bud development or slightly reduced growth.

Perhaps the safest course to ensure plant adaptability is to grow plants native to your particular region. Such plants most likely have the constitution to survive in your garden. And for the most part, local nurseries stock only plants that are known to survive in their region. However, plants don't stay in their regions of origin any more than gardeners do. Plants native to China, Siberia, or Mexico thrive alongside each other in many U.S. gardens. Furthermore, a gardener in California may want to grow a plant native to the Great Plains. New plants that no one knows a lot about constantly debut on the retail market, and gardeners always want to experiment. In these cases, gardeners need some way to compare their gardens' climates with the climate where the plant grows well. Zone maps play a critical role here.

Most often, when people refer to their growing zone they're talking about which USDA zone they live in.

The USDA Plant Hardiness Zone Map

The U.S. Department of Agriculture's Plant Hardiness Zone Map — last updated in 1990 — is the most widely used hardiness zone map. The map has been so useful for gardeners in the United States that the system has been extended to other regions, such as Europe. The USDA zone map is the one most gardeners in the United States rely on, and the one that most garden magazines, catalogs, and books currently use. You can find a copy of the map at www.usna.usda.gov/Hardzone/. or in the full-size vrsion of *Gardening For Dummies,* 2nd Edition.

The chill factor

The USDA zone map divides North America into zones based on the average annual minimum temperature. Each zone is 10°F (–12°C) warmer (or colder) in an average winter than the adjacent zone.

North America encompasses 20 zones, numbered 1 through 11. (Zones 2 through 10 are subdivided into *a* and *b* regions where average minimum temperatures differ by 5°F, or –15°C. We don't include the subzones in this book because these designations exist only for North America.) Western Europe has ten zones (numbered 1 through 10).

These zone maps link regions that share an average winter minimum temperature. For instance, typical winters in Colorado Springs, Colorado, and Albany, New York, reach

–20°F (–29°C), so each city is in USDA Zone 5. This is not to say that the climate in these distant cities is the same or that the same plants grow well in both cities. But the average winter minimum temperatures are very similar, and that is one of the key factors that determines plant survivability.

All the plants in this book bear the code for a USDA hardiness zone. If you live in one of the plant's recommended zones, you have some assurance that the plant is hardy enough to survive winter.

USDA zone shortcomings

Unfortunately, no zone map is perfect, and the USDA hardiness map is no exception. In the eastern half of North America, the USDA map doesn't account for the beneficial effect of a snow cover over perennial plants; the regularity or absence of freeze-thaw cycles; or soil drainage during cold periods. Other factors that determine plant survival that this zone map can't accommodate include the amount and distribution of rainfall (or availability of irrigation water) and soil conditions.

In the western United States (west of the 100th meridian, which runs roughly through the middle of North Dakota and South Dakota and down through Texas, west of Laredo), the USDA map is even less useful. The key problem is the map's absolute reliance on average winter minimum temperature — a system that can equate regions of climates that differ in every way but temperature, such as San Diego and Florida. If you live in the West, try to have a copy of the Sunset Western Climate Zone Map handy. Check out this chapter's "Sunset zone information for westerners" sidebar to find out more about the Sunset system.

The American Horticultural Society's Plant Heat-Zone Map

The significance of winter's lowest temperatures decreases as we shift from places where winter freezes can kill many plants to areas where freezes merely mean frost on lawns and windshields. Obviously, winter lows above 20°F (–6.6°C), and especially lows in the high 20s, are much less damaging than lower temperatures. But on the other hand, areas with mild winter temperatures often have soaring summer temperatures. Gardeners have discovered that summer high temperatures can limit plant survival just as surely as winter low temperatures can.

In 1997, the American Horticultural Society published a zone map that accounts for a plant's adaptability to heat. Called the *AHS Plant Heat-Zone Map* (or the *Heat Map*), this 12-zone map of the United States indicates the average number of days each year when given regions experience temperatures of 86°F (30°C) or higher. According to the AHS, 86°F is the temperature at which many common garden plants begin to suffer damage from heat. The zones range from summer cool zone 1 (one day or less per year at 86°F or warmer) through hot summer zone 12 (210 days or more per year at 86°F or warmer).

Sunset zone information for westerners

Average minimum temperature, as depicted in the USDA zone map, isn't the only factor that determines which plants grow in particular locations, but it is a fairly accurate predictor in many regions. In western North America, however, the weather comes in from the Pacific Ocean and becomes less *marine* (stable) and more *continental* (subject to wide swings) as it moves from mountain range to mountain range. In these areas, summer heat, the amount and duration of precipitation, humidity, seasonal winds, and the number of sunlight hours affect plant hardiness as much as, or more than, winter cold.

If you live in western North America, we suggest that you check out the zone maps featured in the *Sunset Western Garden Book* (Sunset Publishing Corp.). This zone system is based on what plants grow where rather than on a single feature of climate, such as minimum temperature. Many garden experts have contributed to the Sunset zone maps over the years, so these zones reflect the plants that thrive there. You can also check out this zone system at the *Sunset* Web site (go to www.sunset.com, click on "Garden," and under "Sunset Climate Zones," click on "Find Yours.").

To find out more information about the map and to download your own copy, head to www.ahs.org/publications/heat_zone_map.htm. You can also buy your own color poster of the AHS map for $9.95. To order, call the AHS at 800-777-7931, ext. 124.

Length Counts: How Long Is Your Season?

You can grow most vegetables and annual flowers anywhere! Some of the largest, most beautiful vegetables we've ever seen were from avid gardeners in Alaska. If you can grow vegetables where the sun doesn't shine for six months of the year, you know they're easy to grow.

Which USDA zone you live in isn't as critical for vegetable growing as it is for fruits, perennial flowers, trees, and shrubs. When it comes to vegetables and other annuals, the length of your growing season is much more important.

A *growing season* consists of the *average* number of days between frosts. Sometimes you hear growing season referred to as *frost-free days*. Some vegetables are very quick to grow and mature, so they require relatively little time. Others need a long growing season. Usually, seed packets or garden catalogs show a number along with the phrase *days to harvest* or something similar. This number is a rough guide to how long a season that particular vegetable needs to mature. Of course, it would make no sense for us here in Burlington, Vermont, to grow a vegetable that requires 200 frost-free days to mature, like jicama for instance. It'd never have a chance! Likewise, to grow many kinds of tomatoes to maturity here, we need to start seeds indoors before the last frost. This early start means 1- to 2-month-old plants are ready for planting as soon as the danger of frost passes. Table 2-1 shows USDA zones and typical frost-free days.

Table 2-1   Typical Number of Frost-Free Days by USDA Zone (Northern Hemisphere)

Zone	Last Frost Date	First Frost Date	Typical Number of Frost-Free Days
Zone 1*	June 15	July 15	30
Zone 2	May 15	August 15	90
Zone 3	May 15	September 15	120
Zone 4	May 10	September 15	125
Zone 5	April 30	October 15	165
Zone 6	April 15	October 15	180
Zone 7	April 15	October 15	180
Zone 8	March 10	November 15	245
Zone 9	February 15	December 15	265
Zone 10	January 20	December 20	335
Zone 11	Frost-free		365

Susceptible to frost all year

As a general rule, if you plant your tomatoes, cucumbers, and watermelons in May or June and your broccoli, lettuce, and peas a month or so before that, you're doing okay.

Stretching Your Garden Season

When you live in a northern climate, you deal with a short growing season. If you want to increase your garden bounty, you need to squeeze in a few extra weeks of plant growth earlier and later in the year. By using some of the techniques described here, you can enjoy the advantages that gardeners have in one or two zones milder.

Planting earlier in the year

Gardeners are master manipulators and have devised all sorts of ways to get a jump on spring. The first simply is to plant early. Here's how to get away with fooling Mother Nature:

- ✔ **Start plants indoors.** Cool-season plants, such as snap-dragons or lettuce, tolerate light frosts. Start them indoors, timed so that they are ready for transplanting about three to four weeks before the average last frost date.

  You can start frost-tender plants — such as marigolds — early, too. Plan to transplant them under protective cover (described in this section) about two weeks before the average last frost date.

- ✔ **Use a cold frame.** A *cold frame* speeds seed germination and shelters plants from frost. The frame is a bottomless box, usually constructed from wood. The structure has a slanting, tight-fitting top made of old windows or other transparent or translucent materials such as plastic or fiberglass. A typical frame is approximately 3 feet wide and 6 feet long (1 x 2 m) with an 18-inch-high (30 cm) back sloping down to 12 inches high (46 cm) in the front (see Figure 2-1).

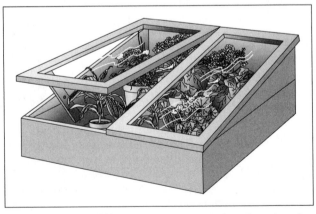

Figure 2-1: Use a cold frame to protect young plants in early spring.

Place the frame outdoors, over a garden bed or against the south wall of your home. Orient the frame so that it slopes to the south. The sun warms the air and soil inside, creating a cozy environment for plants. Sow seeds for transplants directly in the cold frame. (Or grow crops such as radishes, spinach, beets, and lettuce to maturity in the frame.)

Prop the top open during the day for ventilation and lower it at night to conserve heat. If you can't check the frame regularly, consider buying a thermostatically controlled vent opener as insurance against cooking or freezing your plants.

If you like the idea of a cold frame but want even greater temperature control, consider a *hot bed.* This device is essentially a cold frame with a heat source (commonly electric heating cable) to warm the soil. The cable usually includes a built-in soil thermostat preset for about 75°F (24°C), ideal for germinating most seeds. You can find cable with a thermostat and plug sold by wattage and length.

When tender plants are ready for the garden, you need to protect them from frost. Here's a rundown of useful frost guards:

- ✔ **Use hot caps.** These devices are individual covers that work like miniature greenhouses. Hot caps can be home-made or store-bought. To make your own, cut the bottom out of a plastic gallon milk jug. Anchor it in the ground with a stake and leave the cap off so that your plant doesn't bake inside. Commercially produced hot caps are made of translucent wax paper, plastic, or fiberglass.

- ✔ **Set up a water-filled cloche.** A couple of different kinds are available — one with thin, plastic, flexible walls and one with heavier, stiff walls. In both cases, you fill the walls with water. During the day, the water absorbs solar heat. As the water cools at night, it releases heat slowly, protecting the plant inside from temperatures as low as 16°F (–9°C). Use cloches to protect seedlings from late spring frosts.

- ✔ **Use row covers.** Drape lightweight synthetic fabrics, called *floating row covers,* over the plants (see Figure 2-2). The covers let light and water pass through while protecting plants from temperatures as low as 24°F (–4.5°C), depending on the fabric used. The fabrics are available in a variety of widths and lengths.

Figure 2-2: Lay lightweight row covers directly over seedlings or support them with wire hoops. Plastic row covers develop more heat and must be vented.

Row covers of slit plastic are cheaper but usually require more work because they need support from hoops or a frame. You also have to pull the plastic aside to water. Plastic covers create higher daytime temperatures than fabric, which may be advantageous when you're trying to give heat-loving plants like peppers a boost in cool weather.

✔ **Recycle junk from your house.** Every so often, an unexpected late-spring frost catches you off guard. Usually, the frost prediction comes about the time green, tender, young plants dot the garden. To save plants, rummage around for anything that may protect them without crushing them. Cardboard boxes, old sheets, empty buckets, or even newspaper spread over the plants lend a few degrees of protection. Just remember to remove the stuff the following day or the plants may bake.

In addition to providing frost protection, serious cold-climate gardeners often warm the soil in early spring before planting. They spread a soil-warming, plastic-type mulch over the soil surface and cut holes in it for the transplants. After planting, they protect plants with floating row covers.

Clear plastic traditionally has been the mulch of choice for heating the soil, but weeds really thrive under it. Now you can use a new high-tech option called *IRT mulching film.* This green film heats up the soil as well as clear plastic does, but blocks the portion of the light spectrum that supports weed growth. (Clear plastic is still the best to use if you want to *solarize* or heat the soil sufficiently to destroy insects, fungi, and weed seeds. This technique is most effective in hot summer regions that have many consecutive sunny days.)

Gardening beyond autumn

Now that you have a jump on spring, consider these tips on foiling the first frosts of autumn:

- ✔ **Cover up again.** You often can face an occasional light frost before the first big killer. On those crisp, clear evenings when a light frost is forecast, throw a few bed sheets or floating row covers over tender crops. With a little effort, you can prolong the harvest of summer crops.

- ✔ **Spray on frost protection.** What if you forget — or are just too tired — to cover up crops on a chilly evening? Well, you have a second chance to save them (after you've rested, of course). Turn on your garden sprinkler during the late-night hours (as soon as the temperature drops below 33°F/0.5°C). Leave the water on until the sun has warmed the air above freezing. A fine spray of water is more effective than large water droplets.

- ✔ **Plant again.** Cool-season plants tolerate frost. You can plant a second crop of many flowers and vegetables in mid- to late summer for a late autumn or winter. These plants grow quickly in the still-warm soil of summer and start maturing about the time tender crops are declining. Kale (both edible and ornamental), beets, chard, pansies, and turnips are among the stars of the post-frost harvest.

Gardening all year

Frost is the culprit that usually dictates the beginning and end of the gardening season. Planting dates revolve around the first and last average frost dates. If you don't know the dates for your area, ask a nursery professional or call your extension office. The extension system phone number is usually listed in the phone book among the state university numbers or under "Extension" in the business section.

In mild-winter regions, where an occasional light frost is as bad as it gets, the best way to stretch the season is to keep gardening right through winter. Winter gardening has many benefits:

- ✔ Pest and disease problems are fewer.
- ✔ You don't have to water much, if at all.
- ✔ Winter crops are varied, nutritious, and delicious.

In addition to the cool-season vegetables, annual flowers such as pansies, calendula, stock, and primrose thrive in winter. Autumn is prime planting time for winter gardening, although you can plant some crops, such as lettuce and beets, in succession through the winter.

If you want to reap every last tomato in autumn but don't want to hassle with protecting individual plants from frost, you have a couple other options:

- ✔ **Pick your green tomatoes right before the first frost.** Arrange them in a single layer on a shelf or table and cover them loosely with newspaper. Check frequently for ripeness and toss any that start to rot.

- ✔ **When frost is predicted, cut or pull your plants and pile them together.** Cover the pile with plastic. The tomatoes will continue to ripen.

One strategy for getting ripe tomatoes, eggplants, peppers, and melons before the frost gets them is to grow what are called *short-season* or *early* varieties. These plants mature more quickly than their long-season relatives. An 'Ichiban' Japanese eggplant, for example, takes only 61 days to mature, whereas the Italian heirloom, 'Rosa Bianca,' takes 75 days.

Maximizing Winter Hardiness

You may be better off if you stick with plants that are known to be hardy in your area. If you do, you don't have to fuss with various measures intended to help plants survive. But gardeners often experiment, or perhaps you just want to grow a particular plant that is not reliably hardy in your area. In such cases, you may have to take some special steps to protect the plant against the winter cold.

Gardeners can, to some degree, help plants adapt to winter. For instance, reduce the amount of nitrogen fertilizer applied after mid-July and stop all fertilization by late summer. Also, do everything you can to ensure that your plants enter the autumn season healthy but not growing too fast.

Make sure the soil in which evergreens are growing is well-watered in mid- to late autumn, before the soil freezes. If the landscape where evergreens are located is in a dry site, in sandy soil, or under the overhang of a roof, also make sure the soil is well-watered in midwinter if the temperature is above freezing.

Here are some other steps you can take to decrease the likelihood of winter injury to plants:

- ✔ **Plant on the north side.** Choose a location for marginally hardy plants with a northern or eastern exposure rather than south or southwest. Plants facing the south are more exposed to the sun on warm winter days and, thus, experience greater daily temperature variation.

- ✔ **Mulch.** Apply a layer of mulch, 3 to 4 inches (7.5–10 cm) deep, after the soil freezes to keep the soil cold rather than protect the soil from becoming cold. This practice reduces injury from plant roots' *heaving* (coming out of the soil) because of alternate freezing and thawing. Plants that benefit from this practice include perennials, alpine, rock garden plants, strawberries, and other shallow-rooted plants. A mulch maintains a more even soil temperature and retains soil moisture.

Apply bark products, composts, peat moss, pine needles, straw, hay, or any one of a number of readily available materials from the local garden center. You can prop pine boughs (or remains from Christmas trees) against and over evergreens to help protect against damage by wind and sun.

✓ **Wrap with twine.** Plants such as arborvitae, juniper, and yew often suffer damage from the weight of snow or ice. Prevent plant breakage by fastening heavy twine at the base of the plant and winding it spirally around and upward to the top and back down in a reverse spiral. This technique is more necessary as plants become larger and begin to open at the top. Be certain to remove the twine during the growing season.

✓ **Use burlap screen.** Stretch a section of burlap around three stakes to protect young or not fully hardy plants from the south, west, and windward exposures.

A burlap wrap with stakes protects plants from the drying winter sun and wind and drift from deicing salts applied to drives and streets. Wrap most of the plant, but leave some of the top of the plant exposed. Evergreen plants need light, even in winter.

✓ **Prevent drying.** Narrow and broadleaf evergreens lose moisture through their leaves in winter. Plant roots can't absorb moisture from the soil in winter because the soil may be frozen and, therefore, unable to replace the moisture the leaves lose. The foliage desiccates, turns brown, and may drop. This situation can be serious with evergreen azalea, holly, boxwood, and rhododendron. Make sure that evergreens are properly watered throughout the growing season and into the fall. Decrease watering slightly in fall to encourage hardening off, and then water thoroughly in October and continue until soil freezes.

✓ **Prevent animal damage.** Some landscape plants, especially during a time when there is an extended period of snow cover, become a food source for rabbits, mice, or voles. When their normal food supply is covered with ice or snow, rodents turn to the bark and young stems of apple, flowering crabapple, mountain ash, hawthorn, euonymus, and viburnum, among others. If the animals chew the bark completely around the plant and cause it to girdle, the plant may die. In *girdling,* the all-important living cells of woody plants are just under the bark. If these cells are damaged or destroyed, the water and nutrients flowing between the plant's roots and leaves become impeded or stop completely. Partial girdling creates wounds for borers and disease organisms to enter, and weakens the plant itself.

Protect stems and trunks of these plants in late autumn with plastic collars cut in a spiral fashion so that they can slip around tree trunks. Spray or paint trunks, stems, and lower limbs with rodent repellents. A number of these materials are available in most garden centers. Repeat the application at least once during a warm period in midwinter. Mixing the repellents with an anti-transpirant often results in extended effectiveness of these products. If you use any kind of long-lasting wrap, be sure to remove it come spring.

Chapter 3

Tools of the Trade

● ●

In This Chapter

▶ Looking at the seven most essential and the five handiest hand tools

▶ Finding the right lawn mower

▶ Using string trimmers

▶ Getting to know tillers and garden grinders

▶ Knowing where — and how — to shop for garden tools

● ●

Gardening really doesn't require a shed full of tools. In fact, we recommend starting with just a few essential tools and then building your collection as specific jobs call for more-specialized tools. But having the right tool for the job often makes the difference between a pleasurable experience and a frustrating chore, or between a job well done or not. That's what this chapter is all about: choosing the right tool for the job.

Hand Tools

To save money over the long haul, buy high-quality, durable tools. Generally, forged-steel tools hold up better than welded types. Relatively new on the market are tools with fiberglass handles, which are stronger than wood. Hardware stores and garden centers offer what you need to get started. Mail-order garden-supply catalogs offer more-specialized tools. A good one to try is A. M. Leonard, Inc., 241 Fox Dr., Piqua, OH 45356-0816 (phone: 800-543-8955; Web: www.amleo.com).

The magnificent seven tools

Following is a list of the tools that you absolutely must have:

- **Garden hose:** Buy a top-quality hose with a lifetime guarantee. A good hose coils easily, resists kinking, and remains flexible even in cold weather. Choose one long enough to reach all corners of your garden.

- **Hand trowel:** A hand trowel is important for transplanting seedlings, scooping soil into containers, and doing close-up weeding jobs. Buy one that fits your hand and is light enough to be comfortable.

- **Hoe:** Forgo the conventional garden hoe designed to chop at the soil; buy a *scuffle hoe* instead. This type of hoe is easier to use — instead of chopping, you push the hoe along the soil's surface. A scuffle hoe is indispensable for weeding on packed, level surfaces such as garden paths. Although scuffle hoes vary in design, all work with a push-pull motion. Some cut and scrape the tops off weeds on both strokes. Our favorite, the *oscillating* or *action hoe,* has a hinged blade that moves back and forth as it cuts.

- **Lawn rake (see Figure 3-1):** Nothing works better than a bamboo, polypropylene, or metal rake with long, flexible tines for gathering up lawn clippings, leaves, and even small rocks on both paved and natural surfaces.

- **Pruners:** When you own a pair of pruners that you can hold comfortably and that produces a clean cut with little effort, you'll find it hard to imagine gardening without them. Most gardeners favor *bypass pruners,* which cut like scissors. *Anvil pruners,* which cut by pressing a blade into a soft metal anvil, are less expensive. Use either type to cut soft and woody stems up to about ½ inch (1.3 cm) thick. Use this tool to clip flowers, harvest vegetables, groom shrubs, and prune trees.

- **Shovel (refer to Figure 3-1):** A regular round-nose shovel is the single most versatile tool you can own. You need it for digging, turning, and scooping. When used in a chopping motion, the shovel effectively breaks up clods of earth. Choose a length and weight that's comfortable.

Figure 3-1: The lawn rake is effective for gathering leaves and lawn clippings. The round-nose shovel can dig, scoop, turn, and chop. A stiff-tined rake is useful for spreading and leveling soil.

✔ **Stiff-tined rake (refer to Figure 3-1):** The first rake you should buy is a *stiff-tined* or *steel-bow rake.* This rake is an important tool for spreading and leveling soil and for gathering organic materials. The rake also is a good tool for breaking up small clods of earth. Use both the *tines* (the thin, pointed prongs) and the back edge of the rake for building and smoothing raised garden beds. Keep the tines facing downward when breaking up lumps of soil or collecting stones, and keep the flat edge of the head downward when leveling.

Hand-tool maintenance

Take care of your hand tools — they'll last longer and work better. Try to clean and dry your tools each time you finish your gardening chores, but also know that primary maintenance consists of keeping

- ✔ Wood handles smooth and sound.
- ✔ Metal tool heads rust-free.
- ✔ Blades sharp.

When wooden tool handles show wear, sand off the factory varnish and apply boiled linseed oil. Apply several coats, allowing the oil to soak in each time. Clean metal tool heads with a wire brush and sharpen edges with a file. Protect the metal by coating with rustproof primer followed by a coat of rustproof paint. Many bypass pruners have replacement cutting blades that are easy to install. You can also sharpen pruners (the beveled side of the curved blade only) with a fine-grit diamond file.

Replace worn hand-tool grips with a liquid plastic, sold in most hardware stores. The best tool lubricants are synthetic oils that lubricate, repel dust, protect against rust, and leave only a light film. Our favorite is Corona's CLP Shear Maintenance Oil, available from A. M. Leonard (www.amleo.com).

Five more tools to buy

After you invest in the seven essential tools — and if you still have space in your shed or garage — here's what to buy next. Though not as critical as the seven essential tools, these all-purpose tools are very useful to most gardeners. Which tools you need to own depends entirely upon the jobs that you're trying to accomplish. If, for example, you've just moved into a home with a garden that includes massive, overgrown shrubs, buy loppers before a trowel.

✔ **Garden cart:** A lightweight, well-balanced cart that maneuvers easily makes daunting tasks a cinch. With a cart, you can haul big, heavy loads of soil, compost, plants, containers, or wood with little effort.

✔ **Gardening gloves:** Sooner or later, you'll wish you had a good pair of gloves. Gloves should fit well and be thick enough to protect your hands, yet not so clunky that you can't maneuver small objects. Cloth gloves with leather reinforcement hold up well to general garden tasks. Gloves with extra-long cuffs help protect your wrists from branches and thorns.

Glove materials and their best uses are

- **Cotton/polyester and leather:** Performing general garden chores

- **Synthetics such as Spectra and Kevlar:** Working with saws and knives

- **Latex or PVC:** Working with and around water

- **Chemical-resistant nitrile or neoprene:** Working with chemicals

✔ **Lopping shears:** When you get serious about pruning trees and shrubs, loppers are a must. These tools cut easily through branches an inch or more in diameter. Figure 3-2 shows a pole lopper, which allows you to prune branches that are well above your head.

✔ **Tape measure:** A metal tape measure is essential for laying out garden beds and helpful in spacing plants. When staking out an entire landscape, a 100-foot (30 m) length helps you measure precisely.

✔ **Water wand:** This hose-end attachment is great for watering containers, garden seedlings, and seedbeds. Choose one with a shutoff valve. The wand should provide a full but gentle flow that doesn't wash away soil and seeds.

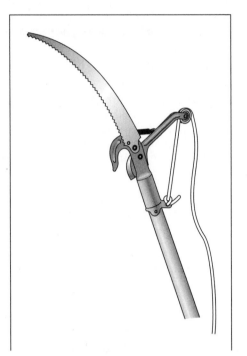

Figure 3-2: A pole lopper allows you to prune branches above your head.

Powering Up Your Tools

Which is it for you: "That cursed internal combustion contraption!" or "Praise be the internal combustion!" Does anyone really *need* power equipment of some kind? In our experience, most gardeners use at least one of these tools from time to time.

Lawn mowers

Lawns may not be the most politically correct corner of the garden, but most of us have one — or wish we did.

One of the reasons that people get fed up with lawns is that lawns require this regular, monotonous maintenance called *cutting the grass,* which may conjure up memories of noisy, dirty, hard-to-start engines. We're here to tell you that times have changed! You have so many more choices now that you're more likely to find the mower that's right for you. New lawn mowers are quieter, better working, less polluting, and safer to use.

Choose a lawn mower according to the size of your lawn, the type of grass, your tolerance (or not) of noise, and your desire for exercise. Allow about an hour to mow 2,500 square feet (232 m²) of grass, using a 20-inch-wide (50 cm) rotary mower. The wider the mower or the faster it moves, the more quickly you can get the job done.

Push-reel mowers

The original teenager's nightmare, push-reel mowers have been rediscovered, reinvented, and improved. Guess what? These mowers are good for the environment and for your body, too. Push-reel mowers are quiet and completely nonpolluting, they give your body a workout that equals a session (at the least) with a treadmill. If your lawn is 1,000 square feet (93 m²) or less and composed mostly of soft grasses such as fescue, Kentucky bluegrass, or ryegrass, this type of mower is a serious option. Most cost around $100, but fancy ones can be twice that.

Power-reel mowers

The power-reel mower is the type of mower that professional gardeners and greenskeepers use. In all cases, the engine drives both the cutting blades and the wheels, but some types throw clippings to the front, and others throw clippings to the rear. These mowers are much more expensive than rotary mowers ($300 and up), but they are unsurpassed at providing a close, even cut — even when you're cutting dense, thick grasses such as Bermuda grass or zoysia.

Push rotary power mowers

Push rotary power is the type of mower that America uses to cut its grass. You provide the push power, but the engine and the spinning blade do the grass cutting. This type is relatively inexpensive ($200–$400, depending on features) and easy to operate. One decision you need to make is choosing between *side* or *rear bagging*. Side-baggers are cheaper; they are slightly less convenient (because you can cut close on one side of the mower only) but work just as well.

Don't buy a push rotary power mower that doesn't include a blade break system, colorfully termed a *deadman switch*. This device makes the spinning blade stop within 3 seconds after the operator releases a lever on the handle. This makes the mowers more expensive but reduces mower-caused injuries.

Self-propelled and mulching rotary mowers

Self-propelled and mulching rotary mowers are basically the same as push rotary power mowers but with added features. Naturally, the price is steeper: $500 to $700, usually. The *self-propelled* feature is plain enough: Pulleys and gears link the engine to the front wheels. The mulching concept is a bit more involved: The mower is basically the same, but the cutting blade and deck are redesigned to cut and recut the grass and leaves, resulting in smaller pieces. These mowers also have no exit chute on the side or rear (or it's optional).

Mulching mowers chop grass blades small enough that the grass filters back down into the lawn. As the cut blades decompose, they release nutrients to the growing lawn, and you don't have to bag and send clippings to the landfill.

Electric rotary mowers

Electric rotary mowers are great, especially if you live next to a hospital or absolutely refuse to deal with anything gasoline-powered. The machines are virtually silent — all you hear is the low hum of the spinning blade. And these mowers are easy to start — you turn a switch, and the blade spins. Electric rotary mowers do have a downside, though. A long cord, usually of a maximum length, restricts your movements (and how much lawn you can cut); the umbilical-free, battery-powered kinds are a bit heavy and pricey. A variety of solar-powered mowers are available now, but these are expensive and not practical in many situations.

Lawn mowers that you can sit on

This category is broad. The simplest are correctly called *riding mowers,* and they do nothing but cut grass. Typically, the engine is in the rear, the mowing deck out in front, and you sit somewhere in between. The mowing deck is 30 to 42 inches (76–106 cm) wide, and engines are 8 to 13 horsepower. Prices range from $700 to $1,000.

Lawn-and-garden tractors are somewhat larger than sit-down lawn mowers and look a bit more like real farm tractors. You sit and look out over a hood that covers the engine, and the mowing deck is right below your chair. Most have a channel steel frame and front axle, and most have 12 to 18 horse-power. These mowers cut 38 to 48 inches (96–120 cm) of grass in one swipe. Some models take attachments such as tillers and snowblowers. Some even offer cruise control! The lawn-and-garden tractor is the type for a homeowner with a large property. Cost? Expect to pay anywhere from $1,000 to $4,000.

Don't buy more horsepower than you need. Lawn-and-garden tractors with 14 horsepower are enough to cut several acres of grass and occasionally till the soil.

Garden tractors are actual, scaled-down versions of farm tractors. Equally heavy-duty as their full-size brethren, their frames are heavy, 10-gauge steel, and both front and rear axles are cast iron. These machines use anywhere from 12 to 20 horsepower and cut 38 to 60 inches (96–150 cm) of grass at once. The benefit of a garden tractor over a lawn tractor is that the garden tractor can accept a variety of attachments, such as rototillers, chippers, and snowblowers. A garden trac-tor is a good tool for a weekend farmer who needs to do lots of chores. Expect to pay at least $3,000 and as much as $10,000.

Trimmers

The string trimmer is (after lawn mowers) the most widely used power tool. Some are electric (power cord or battery), and some are gas powered. Most of the gas-powered kinds use two-stroke engines. This type of engine requires that you mix special oil into the gasoline. A few manufacturers now offer quieter and less polluting four-stroke engines on their trim-mers. Gas-powered trimmers are louder than electric versions.

Most trimmers cut soft grass and weeds with a spinning nylon cord. Some use a solid nylon disk, and some can accept other, heavy-duty cutting blades. For a basic string trimmer, look for one with an automatic or semiautomatic "feed" system for the nylon whip. Some trimmers force you to stop the engine and lengthen the string or whip by hand every time the string wears down.

Electric trimmers

Electric trimmers with power cords are the least expensive kind. These trimmers enable you to work 50 to 100 feet (15–30 m) from an outlet, they're lightweight, and they're quiet. Prices start at about $50. Models powered by batteries allow you to roam more freely but limit you to about 45 minutes of continuous trimming. They cost a bit more, about $100.

Gasoline-powered trimmers

Trimmers with gas power work roughly the same as the electric models, but they give you more power, need more maintenance, make more noise, and let you do more work in less time.

Even though the spinning whip of cord is safer than a whirling blade, it can damage the bark of young trees and shrubs (not to mention hands and feet). If you use this type of trimmer around trees, protect the lower trunk with a heavy plastic collar (available at garden centers). Or better yet, add a ring of mulch around the tree and eliminate the need for close trimming!

Tillers and grinders

Most tillers and grinders (also known as *chipper-shredders*) are hefty machines. Weight begins at about 70 pounds (32 kg) and goes up to a few hundred pounds. Engine horsepower begins at 3, but some have 8 or more. The cost begins at around $500 and ranges upward to $1,600. As big and heavy as they are, both are big time-savers. If you regularly garden a quarter-acre or more, both may be smart investments.

A tiller consists of an engine that provides the power to a transmission that channels the power to the wheels and the tiller. Tillers with the tines in front don't have powered wheels, so the transmission has only to drive the tiller.

If you need a tiller or chipper just once or twice a year, buying your own may not make good economic sense (and where would you store it?). Renting one for a day or two is a sensible option.

All rotary tillers are categorized as either *front tine* or *rear tine*. Front-tine rotary tillers are lighter in weight and cheaper; consider them medium-duty machines. If the soil you're tilling is relatively loose, these are very effective. These tillers, however, are not as efficient if the soil is compacted or rocky. The tines pull the tiller forward; so if the tines connect with a big stone or root, the machine lurches forward. The other downside of front-tine tillers is that you must walk directly behind them, through the freshly fluffed soil.

Heavy-duty tillers have the engine in front and the tines in the rear. Expert gardeners prefer rear-tine tillers because they're much easier and less jarring to operate (even though heavier). The tines dig down into the soil rather than force the machine to lurch forward, and the operator doesn't need to walk through freshly tilled soil.

As the tines turn

Most tines rotate in the direction of travel. The resistance of the soil on the blades causes the tiller to drive itself forward. You need to restrain this driving force to ensure even tilling of the soil.

Tillers offer several kinds of tines, with many different functions. By far, the most common kind of tine is the *bolo* tine, which is shaped like an *L* and is sharpened on the cutting edge. The bottom of the *L* is twisted slightly so that the soil lifts up and away as the tine turns. Some tines are further bent so that they can enter the soil more easily.

The higher the tine speed, the more easily and more finely you can prepare the seedbed. A higher tine speed is also necessary to adequately chop up crop residues or compost and incorporate them into the soil. The common tine speed for front-tine tillers is 100 to 175 rotations per minute. Commercial tillers often allow you to vary the tine speed for different uses. The throttle setting also affects tine speed.

Mini-tillers

Also referred to as *lightweight tiller/cultivators, handheld tiller/cultivators,* and *power cultivators,* mini-tillers are 20- to 30-pound (9–13 kg), gasoline-powered (usually two-cycle) machines. In most designs, the horizontally mounted engine (1–1½ horsepower) sits directly above the tines. Connected to this engine and tine unit are handlebars with a lever for throttle control and an on/off switch. The cost of mini-tillers varies with the number of attachments you buy, but expect to pay around $300.

Mini-tiller tines are made of sharper-edged spring steel and spin faster than the heavier tines of large tillers. The patented Mantis tines are star-shaped, so they tend to slice into the soil. The others have conventional, *L*-shaped tines that dig like a hoe.

On small patches of ground that are in good condition, hand tools are probably just as quick and efficient. Additionally, hand tools are not as damaging to soil structure as tillers, which tend to pulverize particles more than plants need for good root growth. Tillers of any kind may create a layer of packed and hardened soil at the bottom of their cultivating depth — the so-called *plow sole*. But on larger stretches of relatively stone-free ground, the mini-tillers can be worthwhile. They dig about twice as fast as a person skillful with a fork and spade and require much less bending than working the soil with hand tools does.

An automatic clutch activates the tines, which control forward motion. A lever on either the right or left handlebar controls engine speed. At idle, the tines don't move. As you squeeze the lever, the engine speeds up, and the tines engage.

Tines work soil to a depth of 3 to 10 inches (7.5–25 cm). An average working depth after two passes through an average soil is probably about 6 inches, but by working the machine back and forth, you make it dig deeper. Some gardeners use mini-tillers for digging trenches and planting holes for trees.

Here's what you should use a mini-tiller for:

- ✔ Tilling loamy, stone-free soil
- ✔ Tilling soil in small or raised beds
- ✔ Cultivating compacted, weedy soil between rows of vegetables
- ✔ Cultivating soil in narrow, tight locations
- ✔ Weeding in compacted walkways

✔ Mixing compost and amendments into planting beds

✔ Digging planting holes for trees, shrubs, and perennials

Garden grinders

Most garden grinders available today are part chipper and part shredder. The former consists of a 3- to 4-inch (7.5–10 cm) hardened steel blade inserted into the main flywheel of the machine. You feed material — branches or cornstalks for instance — to it via a narrow tube. The shredder part is a larger opening designed to accept armloads of preferably dry leaves. The opening leads to a chamber in which a number of 2-inch-long (5 cm) flails spin and "shred" the material. One manufacturer, Troy-Bilt, currently produces a chipper that is essentially a scaled-down version of commercial, tree-company chippers. Instead of a blade spinning in a flywheel, it has larger blades mounted in a drum. This version has no flails or shredding chamber.

Electric motors, gasoline engines, or power-takeoff (PTO) connections of garden tractors supply power to grinders. Electric grinders are suitable for chipping small prunings up to an inch or so in diameter. Gasoline-powered grinders have 3- to 12-horsepower engines and a manual or automatic clutch.

Garden grinders are among the most dangerous tools that gardeners regularly use. Wear goggles or protective glasses at all times and avoid loose-fitting clothing. Follow all the safety precautions carefully, and always turn the engine off and wait for it to stop completely before reaching in to unclog.

Where to Shop for Garden Tools

All plants are not created equal, nor are tools, potting mixes, and most gardening implements. So to get what you want for your garden — the best quality, a true bargain, or something really strange (like an electric bulb-planting drill) — you need to know where to shop.

By the way, you can order an electric bulb-planting drill from Park Seed Co., 1 Parkton Ave., Greenwood, SC 29647 (phone: 800-213-0076; Web: www.parkseed.com).

Nurseries

In addition to plants and information, larger nurseries offer seeds, bulbs, soil amendments, bark mulches, containers, fertilizers, pesticides, tools, irrigation supplies, and even garden ornaments.

Other sources for tools and garden supplies

Shop at hardware stores and home-building centers for garden tools. Also look to these places for materials to build garden structures, such as lumber, nails, and twine for trellises.

If you live in rural areas, turn to farm and feed stores. These stores are a great source for seeds, tools, soil amendments, fertilizers, pesticides, fencing, and irrigation supplies.

If you know a quality product by brand name or know how to judge the quality of a product, then you are well-positioned to find a true bargain at a discount store. But just because something is inexpensive doesn't mean it's a bargain. Heed this warning: Know what you're paying for.

Shopping by mail greatly broadens your choice of seeds, plants, tools, and supplies. However, besides having to wait for delivery, the downside of shopping by mail is not being able to see what you're buying. That's why it's especially important to know that your sources, especially nurseries, are reliable. Look for the Source icon throughout this book for reliable mail-order catalogs.

Chapter 4

Understanding and Improving Soil

In This Chapter

▶ Clearing a site

▶ Understanding and testing your soil

▶ Improving your soil

▶ Digging and tilling

▶ Making raised beds

*P*reparing your soil is probably the most important step toward bringing your garden to life. The reason? *Roots.* This underground lifeline makes up half of every plant — sometimes more. You may often forget about roots, however, because you don't see them — except for the occasional maple root that the lawn mower keeps hitting. But the roots are there, spreading, digging, and questing for nutrients and moisture.

Before you plant, take some time to get acquainted with your soil. (It's more interesting than you think!) Chances are, you'll find out that you need to make some improvements — typically by adding organic matter (a process called *amending the soil*) and a perhaps a few other goodies, as well. Your goal, as you discover in this chapter, is to create an airy soil, rich in oxygen and nutrients that enable your plants to thrive.

Clearing the Site

The perfect spot for your garden may already be occupied. Whether it's a beautiful sweep of lawn or a patch full of weeds and brush, you need to clear your site of existing vegetation before testing and improving the soil. Follow these steps for clearing a site where you intend to place your garden:

1. **Outline the area where you'll go to work.**

   If you're developing a square or rectangular area, you can establish straightedge lines by stretching a string between two sticks. Leave the string in place or mark the line with a trickle of white ground limestone, spray paint, or flour. For curved portions of the garden, use a garden hose or rope to lay out the line. Adjust the hose position until the curve looks smooth.

2. **Use a flat spade to dig a small trench that establishes the outline of the garden plot.**

3. **Clear the surface by removing plants, sod, brush, and rocks.**

4. **Mow the site to clear the rough ground.**

5. **Cut down woody plants and dig out the roots.**

6. **When the vegetation is down to a manageable level, you can remove the sod and other low vegetation.**

You can use several techniques for clearing the site. If the garden is currently lawn, you can strip off the turf, roots and all, by using a flat spade or sod cutter. This method is hard work, but it does a thorough job.

Stripping sod

Your site clearing process may very well involve getting rid of natural sod. Here's how:

1. **A couple days prior to digging, water the area that you want to clear.**

   Stripping sod is easier when the soil is lightly moist.

2. **If you haven't done so already, mark the edges of the plot.**

3. **Starting at one side of the plot, slip your spade under the grass and slide it under the sod.**

   Don't dig too deep; you want to remove merely the sod and an inch or two of roots.

Another system is to precut the sod into square or rectangular sections and then loosen each section with the spade.

4. **Pivot the tool up, letting the sod flip up over the spade.**

5. **Slice off the sod section and toss it into a wheelbarrow to take to the compost pile.**

6. **Gradually continue in this manner until the garden is free of sod.**

Many garden experts get rid of grass sod by spraying it with a nonselective herbicide, such as Roundup or Finale. When the grass is completely dead, they till it into the soil, adding organic matter to the soil in the process! However, our feeling is that most gardeners are better off avoiding herbicides, even considering the promise of saving time and energy. To use herbicides or not is a decision you have to make for yourself.

If you have a large area of sod to clear, consider renting a sod cutter. These machines are the size and weight of full-size rototillers, so you need a pickup truck or trailer to get one home. (Some rental yards deliver and pick up heavy equipment — of course, they charge extra for this service.) After stripping the sod, stack the strips like bricks into a 3- or 4-foot (1–1.2 m) pile and let it become compost.

Other soil-clearing methods

You can use other ways to clear a garden: Cover it with black plastic or layers of newspapers, or simply use repeat cultivation.

Black plastic

After a month under black plastic, existing plants die from lack of sunlight. Spread the plastic over the entire garden area, securing the edges with spare rocks, bricks, or boards. Overlap neighboring pieces of plastic by several inches so that no light can penetrate. Come back in a month, remove the plastic, and rototill the dead plant matter into the soil. Wait about ten days for errant weeds to sprout. (Because you haven't removed weed seeds, you're sure to get some growth.) Cut down or pull out any weeds that emerge.

Newspapers

To use newspapers, spread a layer of newspapers, five to six sheets thick, over the entire area in the fall. Overlap the sheets about 5 inches (12.5 cm). Use black-and-white newsprint only — color ink may contain lead or other heavy metals. Cover the newspaper with straw or other mulch and leave it alone for one season. After a few months, the sod, newspaper, and other material will have decomposed enough to till under. You've recycled the newspapers, and the decomposed sod adds nutrients.

Repeat cultivation

If you have plenty of time or if your garden is too large for the other site-clearing methods to be practical, then consider the *repeated tilling method.* This process adds good organic matter to the soil and kills existing weeds but takes much of the growing season to complete.

1. **In spring, rototill the garden area and broadcast seeds of a cover crop such as buckwheat, Sudan grass, or black-eyed peas.**

2. **After the cover crop gets to be about 6 inches (15 cm) high, till again to work it into the soil.**

3. **Let the cover crop decay, which takes a couple of weeks during warm weather. Then till again and prepare to plant.**

Meeting Your Soil

Taking time to create a healthy underground environment before you plant goes a long way toward ensuring a healthy, productive garden. You need to know only a few basics and perform some easy tests to determine the characteristics of your soil, and you're ready to start improving your soil like an expert!

To understand your soil, keep in mind what plants need from soil: moisture, air, and nutrients.

Soil texture

Soil comprises air spaces, organic matter, and, mostly, mineral particles. Soil minerals come in three types: sand, silt, and clay. Sand is the largest particle in most garden soils. Silt particles are smaller than fine sand and larger than clay. Clay is the smallest particle. The relative proportions of these particles in the soil determine its texture.

The ideal soil texture is *loam,* which is composed of sand, silt, and clay. Loam soils have the properties of all three mineral types in roughly equal proportions — enough sand to allow good water drainage and air circulation, but enough clay to retain moisture and nutrients. (See Figure 4-1.)

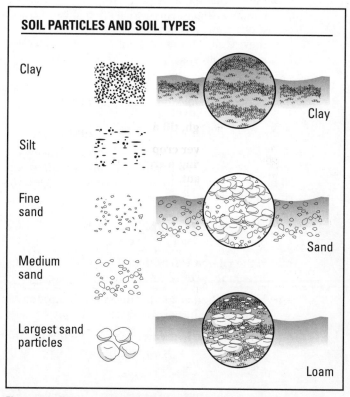

SOIL PARTICLES AND SOIL TYPES

Clay

Silt

Fine sand

Medium sand

Largest sand particles

Clay

Sand

Loam

Figure 4-1: The size of the mineral particles determines a soil's texture. Loam is the ideal soil for most plants.

Most garden soils are best understood as either sandy, clay, or loam. (Silty soils occur but are not common.)

- ✔ **Sandy:** Water drains through sandy soils fast, so it dries quickly. Nutrients also pass through sandy soils quickly. Plants in sandy soils often need lighter, more frequent applications of water and fertilizer.

- ✔ **Clay:** Soils dominated by clay particles are heavy and tend to pack tightly. Clay soil sticks to your shoes and shovel when it's wet, and cracks when dry. Water enters and drains slowly from clay soils, which can make them difficult to manage. On the other hand, clay soils' ability to retain moisture and nutrients makes them very fertile.

- ✔ **Loam:** Loam soils come in many types, but all combine the properties of sand, silt, and clay. A "perfect" loam soil contains 40 percent sand, 40 percent silt, and 20 percent clay. Loam soils have such a good reputation because they're ideal for most plants. But many plants grow well in non-loam soils.

You can use two methods to identify your soil's texture: the *ribbons-and-bows method* and the *jar method.*

A quick test for texture: Ribbons and bows

Get a general idea of your soil's texture by taking a handful of moist soil, squeezing it into a ball, and working it out in a ribbon between your thumb and your forefinger. Stand the ribbon straight up in the air.

- ✔ **If you can't form a ribbon,** the soil is at least 50 percent sand and has very little clay.

- ✔ **If the ribbon is less than 2 inches (5 cm) long before breaking,** your soil has roughly 25 percent clay in it.

- ✔ **If the ribbon is 2 to 3½ inches (5–9 cm) long before breaking,** it has about 40 percent clay.

- ✔ **If the ribbon is greater than 3½ inches (9 cm) long and doesn't break when held up,** it is at least 50 percent clay.

A more accurate test for texture: The jar method

For most gardeners most of the time, knowing the exact texture of your soil is not so important. But when you do know, that information can help explain much of what goes on in your garden. You can then tailor your soil management for maximum effect. Allow several days to carry out the following test.

Here's how to use the jar method:

1. **Put 1 inch (2.5 cm) of dry, crushed garden soil in a tall quart (liter) jar.**

2. **Fill the jar two-thirds with water and add 1 teaspoon (5 mL) of a dispersing agent, such as a liquid dish detergent or table salt.**

3. **Shake the jar thoroughly and let the contents settle.**

4. **Measure the depths of the different layers of soil.**

   When the sand settles to the bottom (in about a minute), measure the depth of that layer.

   Silt settles in four to five hours. You should see a color and size difference between the silt and sand layers; if not, subtract the sand depth from the total to determine the silt depth.

   The clay takes days to settle, and some of the smallest particles may remain permanently in suspension.

By measuring the depth of each layer, you can figure out the approximate percentages of sand, silt, and clay in your soil. For example, you have loam soil if the 2 inches (5 cm) of soil settles down like this: The sand and silt layers are about ¾ inch (1.9 cm) each, and the clay layer is less than ½ inch (1.25 cm).

Soil structure

The way in which sand, silt, and clay particles combine or cluster is called the *soil structure*. Structure modifies the influence of texture. Most often, gardeners use additions of organic matter — compost, peat moss, mulch, and so on — to improve soil structure.

No matter what kind of soil you have, adding organic matter improves the soil structure. Organic matter helps form *humus,* which enables small clay or silt particles to stick together to form larger aggregates; in sandy soils, humus acts like a sponge to catch and hold moisture and nutrients. For more details about humus, see "Exactly what do you add?", later in this chapter.

Two methods of determining your soil structure are the *percolation method* and the *metal-rod method,* which we explain in the following sections.

A quick test for structure: Percolation

The percolation do-it-yourself test evaluates *water drainage* — the ability of water to move through the soil, which is called the *percolation rate.* To evaluate drainage:

1. **Dig several holes 1 foot deep by 2 feet wide (30 × 60 cm) in various places in your garden.**

2. **Cover the holes with sheets of plastic to let the soil dry out.**

3. **When the soil is dry, fill each hole to the top with water and record the time it takes for the water to completely drain.**

   The ideal time is between 10 and 30 minutes.

   • **If the water drains in less than 10 minutes,** the soil will tend to dry out too quickly in the summer. Amend the soil with moisture-retaining matter such as peat moss and humus.

   • **If the water takes 30 minutes to 4 hours to drain,** you can still grow most plants but you have to water it slowly to avoid runoff and to allow the water to soak in deeply.

   • **If your soil takes longer than 4 hours to drain,** you may have a drainage problem. In sandy soil, dig a foot or two (30–60 cm) deep to see whether a hard layer is blocking water movement. If so, break it up in the area you want plants to grow. You may have to dig down with a post-hole digger, though in some cases, the impermeable layer is too deep even for that. You can also use a nozzle on the end of a pipe to make a water jet bore through an impermeable layer.

If your soil is clay, create a raised bed and use purchased soil or a homemade soil mix for planting. The goal is to get plant roots up out of the soggy soil and into well-drained, elevated soil rich with organic matter.

Another test for structure: The metal-rod method

In some regions, particularly ones that receive little rainfall, a concretelike layer lies just under the soil. This layer, which is known as *caliche,* prevents normal water movement and root growth.

In addition to caliche, some soils suffer from a layer of dense, clay soil called *hardpan.* Though not as hard as caliche, this dense layer also prevents good plant growth (see the "Improving Your Soil" section, later in this chapter). The simplest way to see whether your soil has a hardpan or compaction layer below the surface is to take a metal rod and walk around your property sticking it into the ground. If you can't easily push the rod into the soil at least 6 to 8 inches (15–20 cm) deep, you need to improve the structure of your soil. If you push it down and consistently meet resistance at a certain depth, you may be hitting a hardpan layer.

One more big thing: Soil pH

Just to intimidate the rest of us, chemists use a chemical symbol to represent the relative *alkalinity* (sweetness) or *acidity* (sourness) of the soil. This symbol, *pH,* represents the "negative logarithm of hydrogen ion concentration."

Soil pH is rated numerically on a logarithmic scale of 1 to 14, but you'll almost never see a soil with a pH of 2 or 13. In practice, soil with a pH of 4.5 is strongly acidic and a pH of 9.5 is strongly alkaline. Most soils in the world range between a pH of 5 and a pH of 9. An absolutely neutral pH is 7.0.

The correct pH for your plants is important because certain nutrients are available only to plants within a specific pH range. The ideal pH for most plants is from 6.0 to 7.0. A few plants (such as acid-loving rhododendrons and blueberries) prefer more extreme conditions. Usually, areas of high rainfall have a low pH, and areas of low rainfall have a high pH.

Kits for testing pH are available in many garden centers. You can also figure out your soil's pH by using a professional soil test. For a quick check of your soil's pH, try the following fizz tests. These tests are not very accurate, but they can be fun to watch!

- ✔ **To check whether your soil is severely alkaline,** take a tablespoon (15 mL) of dried garden soil and add a few drops of vinegar. If the soil fizzes, the pH is above 7.5. (The free carbonates in the soil react with the acid at a pH of 7.5 and above.)

- ✔ **To check for acidity in the soil,** take a tablespoon (15 mL) of wet soil and add a pinch of baking soda. If the soil fizzes, the soil is probably very acidic (pH less than 5.0).

Your soil, in detail

For the definitive word on your soil's chemistry and makeup, a professional test is the next step. Your local extension office may be able to test your soil or recommend a private lab. The results of these tests can tell you about soil nutrient levels, soil structure, and pH. You also get suggestions on how to make your soil even better.

Keep in mind that the reliability of any soil test depends on the accuracy of the soil sample. Avoid contaminating soil samples with residue from tools, containers, or cigarette ash, for example. The small sample that you send to a lab must also be representative of your garden. Gather soil from several places and mix it together to form a composite picture of the plot. However, don't mix soil from different garden areas where you'll be growing plants with different needs or with soil near foundations or walls where construction residues may remain. Follow the directions from the soil lab or extension office for best results.

Improving Your Soil

If your soil is a nice, fertile blend — one that grows good grass — you may not need to do anything special to it to grow most garden plants. But beefing up the organic content never hurts, because organic matter is constantly being broken down. *Organic matter* — such as decaying leaves, hay, grass clippings, compost, and decomposed cow or horse manure — releases nutrients and other chemicals that make soil fertile and productive. Organic matter is especially valuable for adding richness to sand and lightness to clay. The organic material makes good gardens great and poor gardens better by making any soil more like the ideal loamy soil. Be careful not to use cat or dog droppings, because this waste can contain parasites.

Before planting in reasonably good soil, dig in 1 or 2 inches (2.5–5 cm) of organic matter, such as compost, peat moss, decayed livestock manure, shredded leaves, or decayed lawn clippings. Then, each year, mulch planted areas with an inch or more of compost or organic mulch.

Amending your soil before planting is not always necessary, especially if you're planting long-lived trees and shrubs and if your soil is reasonably good, if not perfect. On the other hand, if you find that your soil is not what it needs to be for the kinds of plants you want to grow, try to correct the problem before you plant. Be prepared to amend the entire planting area so that plant roots can grow freely without encountering a bewildering range of different soil blends. Dramatically different soil types can stop root growth cold. Apply a layer of organic matter, at least 2 to 4 inches (5–10 cm), and till it into the soil.

Plan to maintain your improved soil by adding several inches of organic material each year — even more in warm climates or particularly difficult soils. Here are some tips to improve tough soils:

- **Add a 1- to 2-inch-deep (5–10 cm) topdressing of compost to compacted soils in perennial beds annually.** No need to rake it into the soil.

- **Break up a compacted layer and build extra-deep top soil in annual gardens by double digging (see the "Double digging" section, later in this chapter) or by deeply tilling the soil below the hardpan layer and mixing in generous amounts of organic matter.**

✔ **Build a raised bed if the thickness of the hardpan layer doesn't allow for planting.** (See the "Simple raised beds" section, later in this chapter.) Build the bed about 8 inches (20 cm) high — or even higher if you install a retaining wall. Cover the existing soil with commercial topsoil that's preblended with about 20 percent compost.

Exactly what do you add?

Organic matter that you can add to your soil comes in so many forms and varieties that this book couldn't possibly list them all. Nursery and garden centers offer many kinds, often in 20- or 40-pound (10 or 20 kg) bags. But if you have really big plans, consider buying your organic amendment by the truck-load. By the bag or by the truckload, the following sections cover some of the tempting tidbits that you'll find can do wonders to improve the texture of garden soil.

Compost

When different kinds of dead plant material get piled together, dampened, and stirred or turned every week or so to keep air in the mixture, they become compost after a month (or two or three). Products labeled as compost can originate from all sorts of stuff, but enterprising people who have tapped into the yard-waste stream usually create them. Fallen leaves, shredded Christmas trees, and wood chips left from tree-trimming crews often find their way to compost-manufacturing facilities. Compost ingredients can also include sawdust from lumber mills, peanut hulls from peanut processing plants, and hundreds of other agricultural by-products.

 One place to get lots of compost cheap is from your own city. Many municipalities offer free compost and mulch. Some charge a modest fee for it. The only caveat is quality. Some cities compost industrial by-products that you might not want to have in your garden. Check with your local Department of Public Works.

Expect to find little bits of sticks and other recognizable things in a bag of compost, but mostly judge quality by the texture of the material, which should be soft and springy. If you plan to buy a large quantity of compost, compare products packaged by different companies to find the best texture.

A 3-inch (7.5 cm) layer of packaged compost, worked into the soil, is a liberal helping that should give instant results. To estimate how much you need, figure that a 40-pound (18 kg) bag (that may actually weigh more or less, depending on how it's been stored) covers a square yard (0.84 m²) of bed space.

Composted manure

In addition to its soil-improving properties, composted or "aged" manure also contains respectable amounts of nitrogen and other important plant nutrients. Nutrient content varies with the type of manure. Composted chicken manure is very potent, whereas steer manure is comparatively lightweight. Packaged sheep manure is quite popular among gardeners, and you may eventually encounter some truly exotic renditions based on the waste from zoo animals, bats, and even crickets.

The amount of manure you should use depends on your soil type. With bulky manure from large animals (cow, horse, goat, sheep, elephant), start with a 1-inch (2.5 cm) layer, or about 40 pounds (18 kg), per 3 square yards (2.5 m²). Follow package application rates when using stronger manure from rabbits, chickens, and other birds.

Humus

Bags labeled as *humus* are the wild cards of the soil-amendment world. Anything that qualifies as organic matter for soil, or any soil-organic matter mixture, can be considered humus. Unlike compost, which is supposed to be "cultured" under controlled conditions, humus can come from more humble beginnings. For example, humus may be two-year-old sawdust and wood chips from a lumber mill mixed with rotten leaves and dark topsoil. Or, it could be rotten hay mixed with soil and sand. You just don't know what to expect until you buy a bag and open it up. If the humus has a loose, spongy texture and dark color, and you like the way it feels and smells, go for it. A 2- to 3-inch (5–7.5 cm) layer (40 pounds per 2 square yards/18 kg per 1.7 m²) is a good estimate.

Topsoil

Breaking into bags of topsoil to see what's inside is always interesting. Sometimes the soil is exactly what you might find in bags of humus or compost, and other times it may look more like unbelievably black soil. Whatever the bag contents include, topsoil is almost always cheap. You can use bagged topsoil as a soil amendment, or use so much of it that your flower bed is filled with mostly imported topsoil and only a little of the native stuff.

Peat moss

Peat moss is a very spongy, acidic, brown material harvested from peat bogs in Canada, Michigan, and a few other places. On the plus side, peat moss absorbs and holds huge amounts of water and nutrients while frustrating soil-borne fungi that can cause plant diseases. Peat moss is more beneficial in sandy soil as opposed to clay soils. In sandy soils, the water-holding power of peat is put to good use. Clay soil retains water, so adding peat moss is overkill.

On the negative side, some gardeners are concerned about the sustainability of peat moss harvesting. Peat bogs that are damaged by overharvesting may require a thousand years to regenerate. Because of this, you might want to limit your use of peat moss to situations where it is most valuable, such as creating special soil mixtures for container-grown plants, or for planting shrubs that really like it a lot, like azaleas and rho-dodendrons. We think most, but not all, of the peat moss in nurseries and garden centers is harvested responsibly and sustainably. Gardeners in some areas use shredded coconut husks as a substitute.

Changing pH

If you're growing pH-sensitive plants, or if you're dealing with very acidic or very alkaline soils, you can adjust pH with spe-cific soil amendments. To make soil less acidic, add ground limestone. To increase alkalinity, add soil sulfur. But rather than commit to the ongoing need to adjust pH, consider choosing landscape plants that grow well in your native soil with its existing pH. Amending soil with many kinds of organic matter gradually lowers pH. (Some animal manures tend to have an alkaline effect so should not be used to acidify.) Likewise, most nitrogen-containing fertilizers, natural or man-ufactured, acidify soils — some a great deal, others only slightly. But if your soil pH is significantly too low or too high for the kinds of plants you want to grow, you need to add ground limestone or soil sulfur. To increase or decrease your soil pH, do the following:

- ✔ **Add limestone to raise your soil pH from 5.0 to 6.5.** To each 1,000 square feet (93 m²) of sand, add 41 pounds (18.6 kg); to each 1,000 square feet of loam, add 78 pounds (35.4 kg); and to each 1,000 square feet of clay, add 152 pounds (69 kg).

- ✔ **Add sulfur to lower your soil pH from 8.5 to 6.5.** To each 1,000 square feet (93 m²) of sand, add 46 pounds (20.8 kg); to each 1,000 square feet of loam, add 57 pounds (25.8 kg); and to each 1,000 square feet of clay, add 69 pounds (31.3 kg).

Adding nutrients

If your soil is low in nutrients, which you can determine by having the soil tested or by seeing that plants grow poorly, add extra nutrients. If your soil has been tested, add amendments and fertilizers according to the lab's recommendations. If you haven't tested the soil, add a complete fertilizer according to package directions. A *complete fertilizer* is one that contains nitrogen, phosphorus, and potassium, the major nutrients that all plants need.

Green manure crops and cover crops

One easy way for gardeners to add organic matter and nutrients to the soil is to grow *green manure crops.* These are plants grown to be chopped and tilled or spaded into the soil when they are still green (before they blossom and produce seeds). The succulent plant material breaks down quickly, adding nutrients and improving soil texture. These crops are usually grown during the main gardening season — between crops or just after harvesting a crop. In many climates, green manure crops remain standing over the winter and get plowed into the soil before spring planting.

Cover crops are often the same plants that are used for green manure crops. However, the primary purposes of a cover crop are to prevent soil erosion and to choke out weeds, usually when the soil is bare of crops before and after the harvest.

 The plants used as green manure and cover crops can be divided into two broad categories: *legumes* and *nonlegumes.* Legumes have special nodules on their roots that house nitrogen-fixing bacteria of the genus *Rhizobium.* Examples of legumes are soybeans, vetches, cowpeas, and clovers. If you till the legumes back into the soil, succeeding crops benefit from the nitrogen that the legumes and its *Rhizobium* absorbed from the air.

Although nonlegumes don't add as much nitrogen to the soil as legumes do, many nonlegumes are very useful as green manure and cover crops simply for the organic matter that they add to the soil.

Loosening the Soil

The depth and techniques that you use to loosen the soil depend on which plants you intend to grow and the condition of your soil. For your average garden of annual flowers and vegetables, for example, you can use a process called *single digging* to break up the top 8 inches (20 cm) of soil by using a spade or rototiller.

In existing gardens with light, fluffy soil, you may be able to turn the bed with a spade without too much difficulty and minimize organic matter loss. If you prepare the soil in autumn, let frost help break up the soil clumps. Then spade again in spring and finish up with a rake.

Begin digging by removing a section of soil the width of the bed and the depth of your spade. Place excavated soil in a garden cart or wheelbarrow, or simply pile the soil to the side temporarily. Soon, you'll have what looks like a shallow grave. Next, slice down into the adjacent portion of soil with the spade and roll that soil into the trench you just made. Continue this process until you have covered the garden width (or length). Finally, haul the soil excavated from the first trench and place it into the last space.

When to work the soil

Have you ever grown your own mouth-watering melon, checking it daily to see whether it's perfectly ripe? Preparing the soil is similar. You need to wait until the soil is in the right condition — lightly moist, but not wet. If too wet, clays can dry into brick. If too dry, soil can turn into dust and blow away, leaving beneficial soil life to perish. If your soil tends to be wet and clammy in spring when you're ready to plant annual flowers, you can avoid this frustration by preparing your beds in the fall, when dry conditions often prevail.

Fortunately, the right soil condition is easy to evaluate. Take a handful of soil and squeeze it in your fist. Tap the resulting ball with your finger. If it breaks up easily, the soil is ready. If it stays in a sodden clump, the soil needs to dry out more. If it doesn't cling at all, the soil is dry: Water the area, wait a day, and try again.

After your first pass with the shovel, break up the clods and add the soil amendments and fertilizer. Then dig through the bed again, rake vigorously to break up clods and to mix in the amendments. Use a garden rake to comb through the soil and remove rocks, clods, and any chunks of vegetation or plant roots that you missed previously. Smooth the soil over the entire bed by raking, and you're ready to plant.

Time for a tiller

Digging a small flower bed is a good exercise program, but preparing a large one by hand in one day is almost impossible without the help of a tiller. If you need to cultivate more than 1,000 square feet (93m²), consider renting, borrowing, or buying a tiller. (Of course, exactly how much is too much to do by hand depends on your strength and ambition.) Lightweight minitillers are sufficient for many tilling chores. For larger jobs, look to either front- or rear-tined tillers. Professional growers usually favor the latter.

Another option is to have someone else till your garden. No matter where you live, you can usually find someone in your community who does this for a living in the spring. Look in the classified ads in the newspaper or call local garden centers to find this most valuable resource person. Before the person arrives to churn up your soil, have all the soil amendments on hand that you intend to use. After you or your hired person has tilled the area and raked out the weeds, spread out your soil amendments and fertilizer, and till it again.

Rototillers are a handy tool for occasional use. Beware, however, that repeated use of tillers can create a hardpan layer (known as *plow pan* or *pressure pan*). Tillers promote faster breakdown of soil organic matter because of how they stir and mix the soil; and tillers cultivate soil to only one depth, so the soil beneath the tilled layer becomes compacted from repeated pressure from the tiller.

Double digging

Double digging works the soil more deeply than single digging and is useful for deep-rooted plants or areas where drainage needs improvement. This process takes a lot of work, but the effects last for years.

1. **Mark out a bed 3 or 4 feet (1–1.2 m) wide and up to 25 feet (7.6 m long).**

2. **Across the width of the bed, remove a layer of the topsoil to create a trench 6 to 8 inches (15–20 cm) deep and 1 to 2 feet (30–60 cm) wide. Place the soil in your wheelbarrow.**

3. **With a digging fork, break up the subsoil at the bottom of the trench to the full depth of the tines — about 6 to 8 inches (15–20 cm). Mix in plenty of soil amendments.**

4. **Step down into the bed and dig the topsoil from the adjacent strip, moving it onto the exposed, loose subsoil of the first trench.**

5. Break up the newly exposed subsoil with the garden fork, and add amendments.

6. Continue in this fashion until you break up upper and lower layers across the entire bed. The soil from the first trench, held in the wheelbarrow, goes into the last trench.

7. Spread soil amendments over the entire bed and rake it into the top 6 to 8 inches (15–20 cm) of soil.

After you finish, the earth is mounded up high in the bed. Walk on the adjacent ground rather than on the raised bed. When you go to prepare the bed in subsequent planting seasons, you'll be amazed at how little work it takes to loosen the ground.

Simple raised beds

Raised beds are an ideal way to loosen the soil of the garden and define planting areas. To make a raised-bed garden, outline the beds with string. For vegetable gardens, a 3-foot-wide (1 m) bed is best; for ornamental plantings, choose a size that best fits your design. After you define the beds, loosen the soil in the bed by using a shovel or a garden fork. Then shovel soil from an adjacent path onto the bed. Figure 4-2 shows a basic raised bed and one edged with wood.

Roses, carrots, parsnips, and other deep-rooted plants grow best when you loosen the soil 12 inches (30 cm) deep or deeper. This requirement calls for building a raised bed over the existing garden or for double digging.

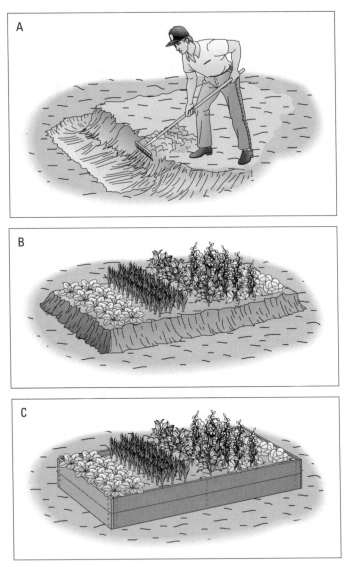

Figure 4-2: Create raised beds by first drawing soil from walkway areas onto loosened soil (A). Leave the edges as they are (B), or finish the edges with untreated wood or other materials (C).

Chapter 5

Choosing and Planting Seedlings, Trees, and Shrubs

. . . .

In This Chapter

▶ Planting seedlings

▶ Working with container-grown trees and shrubs

▶ Knowing what to do with bare-root plants

▶ Getting balled-and-burlapped trees and shrubs into the ground

. . . .

*N*urseries in the same geographic location tend to sell certain types of plants during certain seasons and in certain ways. (Think of fruits and vegetables in a grocery store: Some are available only during specific seasons, and different types may be packaged very differently, each requiring a specific type of cleaning and preparation prior to eating.) Understanding when to shop for your plants and how to plant different plant types is a useful and important gardening skill.

Most annuals and vegetables are available as *seedlings* or *transplants* — the little guys that come in packs or small pots.

Larger, permanent plants — shrubs, trees, and vines, for example — come typically in containers of gallon size to 15 gallons (3.8–57 l) and larger. You can find container-grown plants year-round in mild climates and throughout the growing season in colder regions.

Plants are also available in two other, more seasonal forms: *bare-root* and *balled-and-burlapped.* Each has its own reasons for being and its own special planting techniques. (Of course, you can use other ways to get plants started — like bulbs.)

Buying and Planting Seedlings

In this section, we talk mostly about annuals and vegetables sold in plastic cell-packs of various sizes and in small pots (usually 3–4 inches/7.5–10 cm wide). The same planting advice also applies to seedlings you have grown yourself.

Exactly when plants are available locally depends on your climate. Early in spring and again in fall, expect to find seedlings that grow best in cool conditions. Plants that require warmer weather arrive later on and keep coming as long as customers keep buying.

As you shop, look for seedlings that are a vibrant green color and are relatively short and stocky. Also look around at the display. Has the retailer simply lined up everything in the blazing sun or gone to the trouble of placing shade lovers like coleus and impatiens under benches or shade-cloth? Most bedding plants, including those that grow best in full sun, hold better in small containers when kept in partial shade.

Plants grown in small containers cost less than those in larger ones. Larger plants with more extensive root systems have a head start over smaller plants; however, larger, more developed bedding plants may have one disadvantage. In any container, a plant's roots tend to grow into a thick spiral. If the root system is extremely crowded, the roots may refuse to spread outward after transplanting.

At the nursery, don't be shy about tipping the plant out of its pot or pack and inspecting its roots. Avoid plants with thick tangles of root searching for a place to grow — like out the bottom of the container's drainage hole.

If you buy plants already in flower, pinch off the blossom when you set out the plants. This preemptive pinching encourages the plants to grow more buds and branches.

Figuring Out Spacing for Transplants

Flowering annuals vary in how much space they need to grow. Plant spacing tends to be very tight in window boxes and containers, but in open beds your best strategy is to space plants so that they will barely touch each other when they reach full maturity. Space very small annuals like sweet alyssum and lobelia only 4 to 6 inches (10–15 cm) apart, whereas big coleus and celosia may do better 18 inches (46 cm) apart. Most other annuals grow best planted 10 to 12 inches (25–30.5 cm) apart, more or less. The plant tags stuck into the containers of purchased bedding plants often suggest the best spacing.

Instead of setting your annuals in straight lines, you get better results by staggering them in a concentrated zigzag pattern so that you have two or more offset rows of plants. Better yet, plant different annuals in natural looking teardrop-shaped clumps (called *drifts*). The clump approach also makes many flowers easier to care for. A closely spaced group of plants that need special care is much simpler than a long row when you need to pinch, prune, or water and feed.

You can estimate spacing with just your eyes if you like, and simply go over the prepared bed, making little holes where you intend to set the plants. Or, you can mark the planting spots with craft sticks or lightly dust each spot with plain, all-purpose flour. If you purchased plants in individual containers, simply place each one where you intend to plant it, and move the plants around as needed until you're happy with the arrangement.

Planting Seedlings, Step by Step

Whether you buy your seedlings at the nursery or grow your own from seeds, follow these steps to ensure a seamless transition from nursery to garden.

1. **A day or two before transplanting, water the planting bed so that it will be lightly moist when you set out your plants.**

2. **At least one hour before transplanting, water your seedlings thoroughly.**

   Doing so makes seedlings much easier to remove from their containers.

   Ideal transplant time is any time temperatures are moderate — neither too hot nor too cold, and not too windy. If weather is particularly hot when seedlings are ready, wait for morning or afternoon. If it's mid-summer and you're in a hot climate, try waiting for a cloudy day. Transplanting under the hot sun causes unnecessary stress to the little plants.

3. **Check to see if small roots are knotted around the outside of the drainage holes.**

   If you find roots knotted in such a manner, break them off and discard them before trying to remove the plants.

4. **Remove the plant from the container by pushing and squeezing on the container bottom so that the entire root ball slips out intact, as shown in Figure 5-1.**

Figure 5-1: Carefully remove the plant from the container so that the root ball slips out intact.

If the root ball doesn't come out easily, use a table knife to gently pry it out, the same way you might remove a sticky cake from a pan. For stubborn trees and shrubs, carefully use a strong utility knife to slice through the container. Pull on the top of the plant only as a last resort.

5. **Use your fingers or a table fork to loosen the tangle of roots at the bottom of the root ball.**

   Loosening the roots is important! Otherwise, the roots may make little effort to spread out into the soil.

6. **Make final spacing decisions, and then dig small planting holes slightly wider than the root balls of the plants.**

7. **Set the plants into the holes at about the same depth they grew in their containers.**

   You may need to place a few handfuls of soil back in the hole and then set the plant in place to check the height.

8. **Lightly tamp down the soil around the roots with your hands so that native soil comes in contact with the root ball, as shown in Figure 5-2.**

Figure 5-2: Firming the soil removes pockets of air around the roots.

Tamping down the soil helps remove some pockets of air, which can dry out roots. Keep a watering can handy to help settle soil around roots.

9. **Mix a batch of balanced or high-phosphorous, water-soluble fertilizer and give each plant a good shot.**

   High-phosphorous fertilizers have a large middle number, such as 5-10-5.

   If you mixed in fertilizer while preparing the planting bed, you shouldn't have to fertilize more now. Generally not essential, high-phosphorus fertilizers promote strong flowering. For more about fertilizers, see Chapter 7.

10. **Water the entire bed until it is evenly moist.**

11. **After a few days, check to make sure soil has not washed away from the top of the plants' roots.**

    If the root ball is exposed, use a rake or small trowel to add more soil, making sure the root ball is covered.

12. **As soon as new growth shows, mulch around plants with an attractive organic material such as shredded bark, pine needles, or shredded leaves.**

   A 2- to 3-inch (5–7.5 cm) layer of mulch greatly discourages weeds and radically reduces moisture loss from the soil due to evaporation. It also prevents the soil from forming a crust by cushioning the impact of water drops from rain and sprinklers.

Container-Grown Trees and Shrubs

Most shrubs and trees that you buy these days are in containers — often called *cans* although they're probably made of plastic not metal. This system has several advantages: The plants are easy to move around, and you don't have to plant them right away. (Be sure to continue their watering routine until you're ready to plant.)

Planting your own trees and shrubs saves costs, but planting larger plants requires stamina. Start with smaller, container-grown shrubs that are not too heavy and that can be planted any time the weather is mild. Large balled-and-burlapped trees are heavy and may require a crew of several strong people. Select your plants carefully and calculate placement and hole width and depth in advance so that you don't have to attempt last-minute corrections.

Choosing container-grown trees and shrubs

You want plants that have a healthy appearance — with sturdy branches, dense foliage, and other signs of vigorous growth depending on the type of plant. Inspect the root system as well as you can. You don't want a plant that has spent too little or too much time in the container. If recently planted, the root system may not have developed enough to hold the soil ball together; soil can just fall off the roots as you plant. If the plant has been in the can too long, it may become *root-bound* — when roots are so tangled and constricted, the roots have a tough time spreading out into the soil and growing normally.

Look for these classic root-bound symptoms:

- ✔ Roots stick out the container's drain holes.

- ✔ Roots bulge out above the soil line.

- ✔ Plants are *spindly* (tall but with few leaves), poorly proportioned in relation to the container, or have a lot of dead growth.

Avoid root-bound plants; or, failing this, at least gently loosen and untangle the roots without shattering the ball of soil at planting time.

If a plant is extremely root-bound, slice right through the bottom of the root-bound ball, going up a little more than halfway. Spread open the two flaps over a mound of soil and plant as usual. Or using a sharp knife, slice through the outer roots in several places. This causes the roots to branch out and form new growth.

Transplanting trees and shrubs from containers

Follow these steps for planting container-grown trees and shrubs:

1. **Dig a hole as deep as the original root ball (use a stick to determine depth) and three times as wide as the root ball.**

   Slant the walls of the hole outward and loosen them with a shovel or garden fork to allow easy root penetration. In heavy clay soil, ensure good drainage around the plant by digging the hole 1 or 2 inches (2.5–5 cm) shallower than the depth of the original root ball.

   If you have average or better soil, don't bother to amend the soil that you use to refill the hole; roots may not grow beyond the amended area if you do. If your soil is especially poor, work compost or organic matter such as composted fir bark into the soil that goes back into the hole.

   Locate any underground wires, cables, or pipelines before you begin digging, and proceed around them carefully. You can easily cut through a wire with a sharp spade or fork.

2. **Remove the plant from its container.**

   Most plant containers are plastic, and plants slip right out. If they don't, trim away any roots protruding from drainage holes and water the plant thoroughly. Tap the bottom or knock the rim of the can on a hard surface, and then tip the can upside down (or onto its side, for large plants) and slide out the root ball.

   Most nurseries are happy to take back empty plastic containers, either for recycling or reuse. Some even charge a deposit.

3. **Place the plant into the hole, at the right depth, and fill around the root ball with soil, as shown in Figure 5-3.**

   Stand back and check the plant's position to be sure it's oriented the way you'd like, and then begin backfilling. When you've replaced about half the backfill, tamp down with your hands or the end of a shovel. Water and let the water drain before continuing to fill to the soil level (which is usually the same as the root-ball level).

4. **Water the plant well by letting a hose trickle into the planting area until the area is soaked.**

To help direct irrigation and rainwater to the new roots, shape loose surface soil with your hands into a water-holding basin. Make it 3 to 4 inches (7.5–10 cm) high just outside the root ball.

Continue to water any time the soil begins to dry out for the next six months to a year. Don't count exclusively on sprinklers or rain to water new plants. To see if soil is dry, dig down 4 to 6 inches (10–15 cm) with a trowel. If it's hard to dig, and if the soil is very dry, the root ball needs water.

Figure 5-3: A cutaway view of a container-planted tree.

5. Mulch the plant.

Cover the excavated soil and several inches beyond (the larger the plant, the wider the circle) with 2 to 3 inches (5–7.5 cm) of mulch. After spreading the mulch, pull it an inch or two away from the main stem of the plant. (Sometimes mulch there will promote disease problems.)

6. Stake, if necessary.

Some trees in some situations need support for a year or two until they can support their own weight. Two situations when stakes are needed are if the trunk is very narrow or if you've planted in a very windy situation. Otherwise, most trees are better off without stakes.

To stake a tree, drive a stake or two into the soil beyond the roots. Attach ties to the tree at the lowest point at which the top remains upright. Tie loosely so that the tree can move in the wind and gain trunk strength. Figure 5-4 shows how to stake a tree with a single stake and with two stakes.

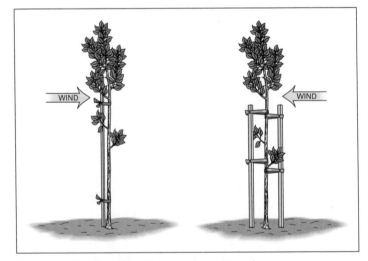

Figure 5-4: Staking a tree with one stake or two stakes.

If using guy wires, establish the lowest point on the trunk where the tree needs support. Use cable or heavy twine to connect the tree from that point to stakes in the soil, as shown in Figure 5-5.

Whatever kind of staking you use, be sure to check once or twice a year to see if it is still necessary. Remove the stakes as soon as practical. Stakes left in place beyond their usefulness are a common cause of tree problems.

A tree with a strong trunk stands on its own without staking. However, if the tree was staked in the nursery or if you are planting in a windy location, proper staking supports the tree during its first year in the ground.

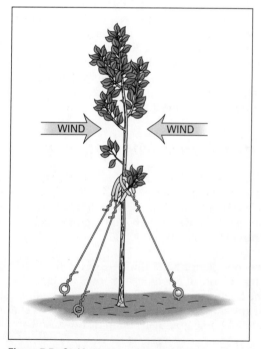

Figure 5-5: Staking a tree with guy wires.

Bare-Root Planting

The tried-and-true method of bare-root planting offers benefits to the plant and to the gardener. During the dormant, leafless season, nursery workers dig up *deciduous* (leaf-shedding) plants and remove the soil around the roots. Bare-root plants are easy to transport and handle — which allows for a lower price than the same plants sold in containers. Bare-root is also a good way for plants to get off to a good strong start; roots can follow their natural direction better than they can in the confines of a container.

Choosing bare-root plants

The most important factor to look for in bare-root plants is roots that are fresh and moist, not dried out and stringy. Check for damaged, soft, broken, mushy, or circling roots and prune them back as necessary to healthy, firm growth. Inspect the top growth for broken branches and damaged buds. Ask a nurseryperson about proper preplanting pruning for the specific plant. Don't let the roots dry out; soak them in a bucket of water before planting, if necessary.

Planting bare-root plants

Plant bare-root plants by using the same procedure for container-grown plants described in the "Transplanting trees and shrubs from containers" section, earlier in this chapter. The only difference between the two procedures is in the shape and depth of the hole you dig.

For bare-root planting, set the base of the roots on a cone of soil in the middle of the hole, as shown in Figure 5-6, adjusting the cone height so that the first horizontal root is just below the soil surface. Spread the roots in different directions and then refill the hole gradually, tamping down soil around roots.

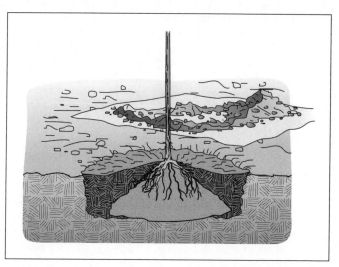

Figure 5-6: Spread the roots of a bare-root plant around a central cone of soil.

Burlap-Wrapped Root Balls

Another time-honored method for distributing plants, particularly evergreen shrubs and trees such as spruce, pine, and fir, is the wrapped root-ball method. During fall and winter, nurseries dig these plants from growing fields and wrap the root balls in burlap (sometimes also wrapping both burlap and root ball in a wire cage for the extra support).

Choosing balled-and-burlapped plants

When looking at balled-and-burlapped plants, be sure to check for major cracks or breaks in the root ball. Make sure that the trunk doesn't rock in the soil ball or move. Keep the root ball moist if you can't plant right away; cover it with organic matter such as ground bark, and moisten thoroughly. Keep the plant in a shady spot until you plant it.

Planting balled-and-burlapped plants

Dig a hole with a circumference twice as large as and a depth equal to the root ball. The root ball should sit on firm soil to avoid settling. Set the root ball into the hole; check the position of the plant, and then remove all burlap, nails, and any twine or wire to prevent interference with the plant's future growth. If you can't remove all the burlap, use a sharp knife to cut off everything except for what is directly underneath the ball. (See Figure 5-7.)

Figure 5-7: Remove any metal, burlap, and twine to avoid inhibiting growth.

To get balled-and-burlapped planting height just right, open the root ball and remove some soil from the top until you find the first *root flare* or horizontal root. That root should be positioned just below the soil surface. Many trees are planted too deeply because they have too much soil over the roots in the root ball.

Shrubs for multi-season color

If it's color you're after, certain shrubs provide it in abundance through a combination of flowers, fruit, and fall color. In other words, these are shrubs that provide more than one season of color. Here are some of our favorites:

✓ **Azalea:** Flowers, fall color

✓ **Barberry:** Flowers, fruit, fall color, colorful foliage

✓ **Cotoneaster:** Flowers, fruit, fall color

✓ **Euonymus:** Fruit, fall color, colorful foliage

✓ **Firethorn:** Flowers, fruit

✓ **Flowering fruit:** Flowers, colorful foliage

✓ **Heavenly bamboo:** Flowers, fruit, colorful foliage

✓ **Holly:** Berries, colorful foliage

✓ **Hydrangea:** Flowers, colorful foliage

✓ **Photinia:** Flowers, colorful foliage

✓ **Roses:** Flowers, fruit

✓ **Spirea:** Flowers, fall color

✓ **Tobira:** Flowers, colorful foliage

✓ **Viburnum:** Flowers, fall color, fruit, colorful foliage

Like many things, burlap isn't quite what it used to be. Don't assume that it will decay in a season or two, where it would be fine to leave in the soil around the root ball. Nowadays, "burlap" is often a coarsely woven synthetic that can take years to dissolve in the soil, if it ever does.

Chapter 6

Growing Food Gardens

· ·

In This Chapter

▶ Making a vegetable garden

▶ Choosing your favorite vegetables

▶ Squeezing in herbs

▶ Getting started with fruits

▶ Looking at favorite fruits and berries

· ·

*I*f you have a bit of farmer in you — or even if you don't — you can get a lot of satisfaction out of growing good things to eat. Vegetables, herbs, fruits, and berries can make your yard productive as well as good looking.

Surprisingly, most edible plants (especially vegetables) are easy to grow. You don't need a lot of space either. Gardening has no rule that says you must lay out vegetables in long rows — many of them grow better in beds. You can even mix vegetables, herbs, fruits, and flowers together and end up with a garden that pleases all your senses.

Planning a Vegetable Garden

Vegetable gardening can be downright simple if you follow a few guidelines. Planting at the right time is key, and to do that, you need to know a little about both the vegetables you want to grow and your climate.

Pay especially close attention to the seasons. (Why do you think farmers are always talking about the weather?) Most vegetables are annuals. Their lives begin and end within the scope of one "season." Exactly when that season begins and ends is the rub.

Seasonal preferences

Regarding season, vegetables are broadly categorized as either *warm season* or *cool season*. Warm-season vegetables like warmth and they don't like cold. Their season is pretty much bracketed by frosts: the last one in spring and the first one in fall. The days or months between those two markers are the season for warmth-loving vegetables such as corn, peppers, and tomatoes (see Figure 6-1).

Figure 6-1: Plant warm-season vegetables after all danger of frost has passed.

Now you can guess about cool-season vegetables (see Figure 6-2) such as peas, lettuce, and radishes: They like cool weather; many also can withstand a little bit (sometimes a lot) of frost.

Figure 6-2: Cool-season vegetables stand up to colder weather, but avoid frost!

The last piece of information you need — before actually planting — is the pattern of cool and warm temperatures where you live and how that pattern relates to vegetables. Chapter 2 gives lots of details about how this pattern works, but this section offers some examples specifically for vegetables.

For most Northern Hemisphere gardeners, the timing is pretty simple: The last frost in spring usually occurs sometime between March and May. Plant cool-season crops a couple weeks before that date, warm-season crops one or two weeks after. The first frost in fall occurs sometime between September and November. Any warm-season crops die then, but cool-season crops keep on growing, sometimes until December.

This pattern however, gets turned around for gardeners in a really warm climate, such as Phoenix, Arizona, or Miami, Florida. The overall weather pattern is the same, with the cool season starting in the fall. But that's when the climate finally cools enough for what the rest of us know as *warm-season* crops.

Similarly, in mild-winter regions, such as much of coastal California, southeast Texas, and the Gulf Coast, the cool-season crops won't grow at all during the hot summers. You have to wait until September or October to get these plants started. And in the far north, the cold season is too severe for much of anything to grow, and the warm (or frost-free) season is relatively cool — meaning you grow just about all vegetables at the same time.

Choose the right location

Most vegetables need six to eight hours of direct sun daily for best results. Leafy greens, like spinach and lettuce, can thrive with a bit less. Fruit-producing vegetables like tomatoes, peppers, pumpkins, and squash need more. Be mindful of nearby trees. Deciduous trees allow much light to pass through in winter and early spring, and cast increasingly dense shade as the season progresses.

If possible, locate the garden so that access to and from the kitchen is easy and convenient — you'll be more apt to notice what needs to be tended and to take full advantage of the harvest.

Vegetable garden calendar

Suppose you live in an area like Kansas City and your last spring frost comes around April 15. (See Chapter 2 for details on frost dates.) A couple weeks before that, you kick off the planting season with three cool-season vegetables: lettuce (because it's easy), carrots (because they're pretty), and broccoli (because it's good for you).

To celebrate filing your taxes, you cruise through the garden center and pick up some tomato and pepper plants. As soon as you get the feeling in your bones that the last frost is a done deal, into the ground they go.

Now it's a beautiful weekend in May. You sow seeds of bush beans, sweet corn, and cucumbers. Stash a few basil plants where you see gaps, and sow some dill seeds where the lettuce didn't come up. Now you have a diversified garden going. Keep it more or less weeded and mulched, and the garden will behave while you're on vacation.

Summer's midpoint has passed, so you start some crops like spinach and more lettuce from the cool-season list and get them going. By the time frost comes in fall, you've had your fill of squash and tomatoes anyway, and the spinach will taste a bit better after being touched by frost.

In many areas, the foundations of houses are drenched with pesticides to keep termites from eating the footings. Instead of growing edible plants right next to your exterior walls where their roots can contact death-wish chemicals, use those places for inedible flowers and shrubs.

Make the garden the right size

Start small. A 20-x-30-foot (6 x 9 m) garden may be average, but a 10-x-20-foot (3 x 6 m) plot is sufficient for a garden sampler that will yield a variety of greens, some herbs, a few tomatoes and peppers, beans, cucumbers, and even edible flowers such as nasturtiums for garnishes.

A 20-x-30-foot (6 x 9 m) garden gives you room to grow a wide range of crops, including some tasty space hogs like corn and winter squash. By growing plants in succession and using 3-foot-wide (91 cm) beds with 18-inch (46 cm) paths, you

should have plenty of luscious vegetables for fresh eating —
even extras for friends.

Designing the garden

The process of designing a vegetable garden is both practical
and creative. You need to give plants enough room to grow and
arrange them so that taller vegetables don't shade lower-growing
types. You also need to be aware of the appropriate planting
techniques that fit the growth habits of different kinds of vegetables. How you will water your garden is also a strong influence on the garden design. And you should also think about
access — how will you get to your plants to harvest, weed, or
water? How will you keep out deer and other creatures?

Following are four basic planting arrangements for vegetables:

- **Rows:** You can plant any vegetable in rows, but this
  approach works best with plants that need quite a bit of
  room, such as tomatoes, cabbage, corn, potatoes,
  melons, and squash.

- **Beds:** Beds are kind of like wide, flat-topped rows of soil,
  usually at least 2 feet (60 cm) wide and at least 6 inches
  (15 cm) high. You can install permanent borders of wood
  or other material, which makes maintaining edges easy.
  You can also concentrate all your amendments and fertilizers in the bed more easily and without waste. Beds
  are ideal for smaller vegetables that don't mind living in
  close quarters — such as lettuce, carrots, radishes, and
  turnips — but any vegetable can thrive. Plant the vegetables in a random pattern in the bed or in closely
  spaced rows.

- **Containers:** Of course you can grow vegetables in containers. In fact, containers are ideal for apartment dwellers
  who may have only a patio or balcony to use for outdoor
  living.

- **Hills:** Hills are best for vining crops like cucumbers,
  melons, and squash. You create a 1-foot-wide (30 cm),
  flat-topped mound for heavy soil, or just a circle at
  ground level for sandy soil, surrounded by a moatlike
  ring for watering. Plant two or three evenly spaced plants
  on each hill. Space the hills at the recommended distance
  for between rows.

Proper plant spacing is a compromise of sometimes competing needs. Gardeners want to squeeze as many plants into the available space to maximize harvest or appearance. Plants need enough physical room (in soil for roots, too) to grow and spread. Also, leave enough space between plants for you to get in to inspect, water, and harvest. Check the catalog or seed packet for mature plant size and planting distance recommendations.

Sketching out your plan on paper can help you purchase the right amount of seeds or transplants and use space more efficiently.

Drawing out the design is a good way to see the possibilities for *succession planting* (following one crop with another) and *interplanting* (planting a crop that matures quickly next to a slower-maturing one and harvesting the two before they compete for space). For example, you may see that you can follow your late peas with a crop of broccoli, and you'll be ready with transplants in July. Or you may see that the garden still has space for you to tuck in a few lettuce plants among your tomatoes while the vines are still small.

Improving the soil

The ideal garden location has loose soil that drains well. If you haven't had your soil tested to determine the pH, do so now. Most vegetables require a pH between 6.0 and 6.8. (See Chapter 4 for more on soil testing and adjusting the pH.)

In most gardens, vegetable garden soil can stand some improvement. Apply several inches of compost or natural fertilizers like decomposed chicken manure over the surface and work it into the soil with a rake.

If your soil is hopeless or if you like convenience, consider growing vegetables in *raised beds* — actually just any planting area that rises above the surrounding ground level. The bed simply can be a normal bed with the soil piled 5 or 6 inches (12.5–15 cm) high, or it can be a large containerlike structure with wood, stone, or masonry sides. Wooden raised beds should be made of rot-resistant redwood or cedar or recycled

Design your garden around a small mowing strip for low-maintenance landscapes.

Oleander *(Nerium oleander)*, here in white and pink, is an evergreen shrub.

'Flower Carpet'; shrub.

'Gold Medal'; fragrant, grandiflora.

'Mister Lincoln'; a hybrid tea.

Cockscomb *(Celosia argentea)*; a warm-seasoned annual.

Bedding begonias *(Begonia semperflorens-cultorum)*; a warm-seasoned annual, or short-lived perennial in zones 9-11.

Floss flower *(Ageratum houstonianum)*; a warm-seasoned annual.

Petunia *(Petunia hybrida)*; a warm-seasoned annual,
or short-lived perennial in zones 9-11.

Green and purple kale
with rhubarb chard.

© DAVID CAVAGNARO

© DAVID CAVAGNARO

Heirloom garden tomatoes come in a variety of sizes, shapes and colors.

plastic timbers. If you put in several raised beds, leave at least 3 to 4 feet (91 cm–1.2 m) for access paths between them.

What to start with

Many vegetables are best started from seeds sown directly in the ground *(direct-sown);* others go in as young plants called *seedlings.* You can grow your own seedlings or buy them. (See Chapter 5 for specifics on raising your own seedlings and transplanting.)

Two of your best sources of information about seeds and seedlings are free: seed packets and seed catalogs. To acquire several seed catalogs for free, you can subscribe to a garden magazine; you will begin receiving a selection of catalogs almost immediately. Or you can mail in the coupons found inside the magazines.

Other sources that you can use, which may be a little bit faster than U.S. mail, are the computer and phone. Use magazines to get Web addresses or toll-free phone numbers.

It's all in the timing

The key date in vegetable planting timing is the average date of the last spring frost (when all danger of frost has passed). Though frost may not always kill your young plants, it is damaging to most kinds of vegetables. If you don't know the date for your region, check with your local extension office or nursery.

Table 6-1 lists "tough" crops that you can plant two to four weeks before the last frost date.

Table 6-1	Frost-Resistant Crops
Direct-sow	*Transplant*
Beets	Broccoli *
Carrots	Brussels sprouts *

(continued)

Table 6-1 (continued)

Direct-sow	Transplant
Dill	Cabbage *
Onions *	Parsley *
Peas *	
Radishes *	
Salad greens *	
Spinach *	

* You can sow these crops again later in the season: in midsummer for an autumn harvest; and, in mild-winter climates, in autumn for a winter garden. These plants also are some of the easiest and best for fall vegetable gardens.

Table 6-2 shows examples of "tender" crops to go into the garden after danger of frost is past.

Table 6-2	Frost-Tender Crops
Direct-sow	Transplant
Basil *	Eggplant
Beans	Peppers
Cucumbers	Tomatoes
Melons *	
Squash	

* In areas with a short growing season, these crops are often transplanted as seedlings to give them a head start.

Raise them right

Successfully planting seeds in the ground hinges on two factors: depth and moisture. The general rule: Plant the seeds twice as deep as they are wide. So you plant really big seeds like beans and squash 1 to 2 inches (2.5–5 cm) deep, medium-sized seeds like corn 1 inch (2.5 cm) deep, small seeds like beets and spinach ½ inch (1.3 cm) deep, and itty-bitty lettuce, carrot, and turnip seeds no more than ¼ inch (0.6 cm) below the surface. You can also buy strips of paper with small seeds glued on at exactly the right spacing. You plant these strips, called *seed tapes,* and eliminate thinning. Most seed catalogs offer seed tapes.

Keep the seeds moist. Water helps soften the seed's coat or shell so that the sprout can break through more easily. Either set up a sprinkler to help keep newly seeded beds moist or cover the bed with an old sheet in between daily watering. As long as the soil isn't clammy (cold and wet), the seeds should sprout within a week.

Whether you set out plants or sow seeds, weeds will appear all over your garden about three weeks after you plant. This occurrence is natural, but you do have to stifle those wild invaders. Get a comfortable pad to sit on and hand-weed right around your plants. Then use a hoe to clear weeds from large areas of bare soil.

After you finish weeding, mulch over the weeded space to keep more weeds from taking the places of the ones you killed. You can use rolls of fabric mulch material, chopped leaves, grass clippings, hay, newspapers covered with enough leaves or grass clippings to keep them from blowing away, and even old carpeting.

Have a happy harvest

If you plant what you like to eat, you'll have to hold yourself back to keep from picking your vegetables too early. Fortunately, most veggies are best when picked on the young side, especially leafy greens, snap beans, peas, cucumbers, and squash. With some other vegetables, especially root vegetables, the old-timers taste better. Wait for carrots to reach full size — that's when they are full of flavor; and tomatoes and peppers are best when allowed to hang on the plants until they're very ripe.

When in question, take a bite! If you don't like what you taste, spit it out, wait a few days, and try again. You'll probably be enthralled with the superior taste of really fresh, ripe vegetables from your own garden.

You Can't Go Wrong with These

Following is a list of ten easy-to-grow vegetables, along with a few tips on planting them and recommended varieties:

- ✔ **Carrot:** Plant seeds several times throughout the growing season, early spring into fall for a continuous harvest. Soil should be loose and deep. Varieties: 'Nantes,' 'Chantenay,' 'Touchon,' 'Short n' Sweet,'

- ✔ **Cucumber:** Wait until warm weather to plant seeds. Varieties: 'Sweet Success,' 'Fanfare,' 'Lemon.'

- ✔ **Green beans:** Plant seeds after frost danger. Bush types are easier to manage, but pole types are more productive in an equal space (because they're taller!). Varieties: 'Blue Lake,' 'Contender,' 'Kentucky Wonder.'

- ✔ **Lettuce:** Plant seeds as soon as soil can be worked — hot weather ruins the plants. Varieties: 'Black Seeded Simpson,' 'Buttercrunch,' 'Deer Tongue,' 'Nevada.'

- ✔ **Onion:** Timing the planting of seeds or the miniature onion bulbs called *sets* can be tricky. Also consider mail-order onion seedlings. Check locally for availability.

- ✔ **Peas:** Sow seeds early in spring as soon as you can work the soil. Varieties: 'Alderman,' 'Sugar Snap,' 'Oregon Trail,' 'Super Sugar Mel.'

- ✔ **Radish:** Sow seeds during the short, cool days of spring and fall. During these times, radishes are perhaps the easiest and fastest vegetable to grow. Varieties: 'Cherry Belle,' 'White Icicle,' 'Scarlet Globe.'

- ✔ **Summer squash:** Sow seeds after weather warms up. Grow bush types to save space. Varieties: 'Sunburst,' 'Yellow Crookneck,' 'Scallopini.'

- ✔ **Sweet pepper:** Plant seedlings in warm weather along with tomatoes. Varieties: 'Bell Boy,' 'California Wonder,' 'Sweet Banana,' 'Gypsy.'

- ✔ **Tomato:** Set out seedlings after the air and soil have warmed up. Tomatoes come in countless varieties; among the best: 'Celebrity,' 'Big Rainbow,' 'Brandywine,' and 'Enchantment.'

Tomatoes are one of those rare plants that actually bene-fit if seedlings are planted deeper than they grew in the nursery pot. Plants will be more anchored and sturdier, and roots will develop along the buried portion of the stem. Pinch off lower leaves, and plant as shown in Figure 6-3.

Figure 6-3: Planting tomatoes deeply provides stability and forces roots to develop along the buried stem.

What about Hybrids and Heirlooms?

As you look through seed catalogs or read seed packets, you may notice the words *hybrid* and *heirloom*. *Hybrid vegetables* are the result of a cross (where pollen from one flower fertil-izes another, resulting in seed) of selected groups of plants of the same kind. Hybrid plants may show what's called *hybrid vigor* — a significant increase in qualities such as early and uniform maturity and increased disease resistance. The increased vigor and predictably good performance make hybrids worth the extra cost to many gardeners.

If you choose hybrid seeds, you need to buy a new batch every season rather than save your own. When hybrid plants cross with themselves and form seeds, these seeds lose the specific combination of genetic information that gave the hybrid its predictable qualities. If you plant seed from hybrids, you end up with a very mixed bag of plants.

At the other end from hybrid varieties are *open pollinated varieties.* These plants are basically inbred lines that are allowed to pollinate each other in open fields. The resulting seeds are pretty predictable, but you won't have the consistency of hybrids.

Heirloom vegetables, like the varieties your grandparents grew, have been open-pollinated for years. Heirlooms are enjoying quite a revival because of the variety of fruit colors, tastes, and forms. Many heirlooms are selected for and perform best in specific regions. If you live where these varieties were grown and selected over many years, then the plants should thrive.

Neither hybrid nor heirloom is necessarily better than the other. Try all kinds of vegetables, especially ones that sound promising to you. Then see what works best, what you like most, and plant more of them.

Squeezing in Herbs

You can always use fresh herbs in the kitchen, so try to squeeze a few into a vegetable garden — or into pots or even a flower garden.

Many herbs are annuals (like marigolds), which require full sun and a long warm season. Some, like chives and parsley, are biennials; and several, such as oregano and thyme, are perennials. Most all herbs grow best in soil that is not too rich and that drains water quickly.

The following are among the easiest and most useful herbs to grow:

- **Basil:** This annual is easy to start from seed or transplants. In short-season areas, sow seeds indoors six to eight weeks before the last frost; plant outdoors, in full sun, only after danger of frost has passed. Plants grow 12 to 18 inches (30–46 cm) high. Pick leaves as you need them; six plants are plenty for most gardeners.

- **Chives:** Start plants from seeds or clumps. Plant in early spring as soon as the soil is workable, in full sun or partial shade. Plants grow about 12 inches (30 cm) high and produce round, pinkish flowers in early summer. Use scissors to snip leaf tips as needed. Divide slowly expanding clumps every three years or so.

- **Garlic:** Start with bulbs from the market, nursery, or mail-order supplier (the latter can provide extensive variety selection). Plant in fall. Separate bulbs into individual cloves; leaving the papery membrane in place. Set cloves pointed end up, 2 inches (5 cm) deep and 3 inches (7.5 cm) apart. Harvest all types in midsummer when the tops are mostly brown.

- **Mints:** These tremendously varied plants all have leaves that are rich with aromatic oils, and all share a love of moist soil. Peppermint *(Mentha piperita)* is a favorite. You can snip the tip of a branch, pour hot water over it, and have instant peppermint tea. Plants grow about 12 inches (30 cm) high.

- **Oregano and marjoram:** We place these two plants together here because they're so closely related and so often confused. Oregano *(Origanum vulgare)* is a 3-foot-tall (91 cm) hardy perennial, and marjoram *(O. majorana)* is a 2-foot-tall (60 cm) tender annual. Both are strongly aromatic and flavorful, but marjoram is a little sweeter and milder. The best way to start either plant in your garden is to buy plants from your nursery or by mail.

- **Parsley:** This herb is so familiar as a restaurant garnish it's possible to overlook how attractive and useful it is in the garden. The rich green of the leaves is a perfect foil to spring daffodils or pansies. Snip or pinch a few leaves whenever you need it for a recipe. Start from seeds or plants, but we recommend the latter because gardeners often have trouble starting the seeds.

✓ **Rosemary:** Gardeners anywhere can grow this resinous, aromatic shrub in summer. But if you live where winters aren't too cold, like zone 8 and warmer, rosemary is a perfectly behaved landscape shrub that you can also harvest for the kitchen and barbecue. Many named varieties of rosemary are available, but all have flavorful leaves and stems. They differ primarily in growth habit: Some trail and some are upright. All have blue flowers and need full sun and well-drained soil. Buy rosemary plants at your local nursery or from mail-order suppliers.

✓ **Sage:** This plant is a hardy perennial *(Salvia officinalis)* that gardeners anywhere can have in their gardens for years. They are ornamental: Several kinds have variously colored leaves, but all have the same distinctive flavor that cooks desire. Sage grows 24 to 30 inches (60–76 cm) high and produces violet flowers in early summer. Plant in full sun and well-drained soil. Start with plants from your local or mail-order nursery.

✓ **Thyme:** These hardy perennials are mostly low growing (a few very low growing). Some are ornamental only with just faint flavor. Most, however, have leaves and stems that are rich with fragrant oils. Common thyme *(Thymus vulgaris)* grows 6 to 8 inches (15–20 cm) high and is the form that cooks prefer. But lemon thyme *(T. citriodorus)*, with its citrus scent, runs a close second. Mother-of-thyme *(T. praecox arcticus)* grows only about 2 inches (5 cm) high and is excellent growing between stepping-stones where an occasional step releases the wonderful scent.

Is There Fruit in Your Future?

If you have just ¼ acre (100 x 100 feet/30 x 30 m) in your back-yard or side yard, you can grow the full range of temperate tree fruits (apples, pears, cherries, peaches, and plums), plus berries and brambles. Of course, your climate will impose a few restrictions. For instance, apples are a problem if you live too far south where winters are hardly cold at all, and peaches are pushing their ability to withstand cold in zones 5 and 6 in the north. Nevertheless, don't think "orchard." Instead, think in terms of a fruit garden — you really need only a handful of trees to get more than enough fruit. One full-grown peach tree, for example, gives you three or more bushels.

Apples are available as true dwarf varieties, so you can plant a large number of individual varieties without outpacing your ability to use the fruit. With careful pruning, you can keep the trees as small as 6 feet (1.8 m) tall. Spaced 2 feet (60 cm) apart — each tree can yield between 10 and 15 pounds (4.5–6.8 kg) of fruit.

Also check with your local Master Gardeners — and perhaps become one yourself. You can learn about the program through your local extension office.

Six steps to a fruit-tree harvest

You don't need to don a tin-pot hat, à la Johnny Appleseed, to grow fruit trees. Just take a look at the following general tips:

✔ **Be patient.** Most fruit trees require at least five to eight years from planting to the first harvest. But if you're in a hurry, plant dwarf trees. They'll bear fruit much quicker.

✔ **Plant varieties adapted to your climate.** Most gardening comes down to matching the plant with your climate and fruit gardening is no different. If you live where winters are 25°F (–4°C) or colder, guess what? You can't grow mangoes. Likewise, if you live where winters never drop below 40°F (4°C), you may not be able to grow apples.

Most deciduous fruit trees, particularly apples, need a minimum amount of *chill,* or number of hours below 45°F (7°C), while the tree is dormant in winter. The chill period helps the tree to grow and fruit well the following season. In the north, this chill requirement isn't an issue, but in southern and western regions, gardeners need to choose varieties that have a low chill requirement. Even though the plant is perfectly hardy and will grow well, check to make sure the variety you choose will also produce a good crop where you live.

Get an agent

Extension office agents are people employed by your home state at county offices. They are gold mines of helpful information for farmers and home gardeners like you (and the information is usually free — you've already paid for it with your taxes). They don't have time to provide individual tutoring but will gladly give you literature on crucial topics like the following:

✓ Average first and last frost dates for your area

✓ Home vegetable garden guide, including recommended varieties

✓ Home fruit production guide, including recommended varieties

✓ **Provide pollinizers.** Many fruit trees need the pollen from a different but compatible variety — called *cross-pollination* — to produce a crop of fruit. Apples, pears, sweet cherries, and Japanese plums are in this category. Exceptions include most peaches, figs, and sour cherries. Apples need cross-pollination, but ornamental crab apples can serve, too, so you can get by with only one apple tree if you live where apples (and crab apples) are abundant.

✓ **Plant in the right place.** A good site means full sun and fertile, well-drained soil. If you live in an area with strong winds, plant trees in protected locations. If spring frosts threaten developing buds and flowers, plant on a gentle slope so that cold air travels downhill and away from the trees.

✓ **Keep trees well watered and fertilized.** Water trees deeply every two weeks. The soil should be moist down to at least 2 feet (60 cm) for dwarf trees and 3 to 4 feet (91 cm–1.2 m) for full-sized trees. Use mulch, such as compost or straw, to help maintain even soil moisture. Apply an organic fertilizer, like compost or aged manure, or a complete commercial fertilizer, like 10-4-4, if growth is poor. But be aware that too much fertilizer can cause bland, soft fruit that is susceptible to brown rot.

✔ **Prune and thin.** The primary objectives of pruning fruit
trees are to create a strong tree form and to maximize the
harvest. Check with local experts or your extension
office for specifics on pruning various types of fruit trees.

Thin the number of fruits that the tree sets after flowering
to get larger, higher-quality fruit and to encourage steady,
year-to-year production. The best time to thin most fruit
trees is when fruits reach ½ to 1 inch (1.3–2.5 cm) in diameter. In most cases, thin to allow 6 to 8 inches (15–20 cm)
between fruits. For apples and Japanese plums, thin to
one fruit per cluster.

Planning a fruit garden

Your fruit garden needs lots of sun, at least six hours at
midday in summer. Orient the rows north to south, if you can.
That way, shade in the morning and evening falls on adjacent
walkways rather than on adjacent trees. Plan to maintain
walkways that are at least 4 feet (1.2 m) wide between rows of
trees. As for aesthetics, put lush, free-growing plants like
peaches and apricots up front. Plan for as long a harvest
season as you can by planting different kinds of fruit. And if
you want fruit plantings nearer the house and among the vegetables, stick to the berries. They rarely need spraying, and
they give you the earliest fruit.

Fruits for the home garden

The following sections describe some good choices for your
mini fruit orchard. We list just hardy fruits — no citrus or
other tropicals, which are suitable only for mild climates.

Apples

Apples are easiest to grow and harvest when you buy dwarf
varieties, which grow 6 to 8 feet (1.8–2.4 m). (See Figure 6-4.)
Plant several varieties to provide a range of flavors and ripen-
ing times. Because apples need spraying more than other
fruits, isolate these trees from vegetable gardens, patios, and
pools. The yield of apple trees is 1 to 3 bushels (35–105 liters)

per tree (late summer through autumn). Some apples are hardy through zone 2.

Scab is the most common disease problem of apples, especially in regions that get plenty of rainfall in summer. The following varieties are immune or resistant to scab, and they have excellent flavors: 'Dayton,' 'Enterprise,' 'Freedom,' 'Gold Rush,' 'Jonafree,' 'Liberty,' 'Macfree,' 'McShay,' 'Nova Easygro,' 'Novamac,' 'Prima,' 'Priscilla,' 'Pristine,' 'Redfree,' 'Sir Prize,' and 'Williams' Pride,'

Blueberries

Blueberries are a good candidate for a hedge because they grow in bushes. You need two varieties for cross-pollination — three or more are better and can extend the blueberry harvest to two months. Some blueberries can grow nearly anywhere in North America if you can provide acid soil rich in organic matter. The yield is 4 quarts (4 liters) per plant (mid- to late summer). Blueberries are productive through zone 4.

Figure 6-4: Comparing the sizes of full-size and dwarf apple trees.

Bramble fruits

Bramble fruits — red and black raspberries and blackberries — are best grown as rambling hedges on large properties or trained to a wall or trellis on small properties. Of the group, raspberries are best adapted to cooler areas, and blackberries can grow in hotter areas. In temperate regions where all types grow, the bramble harvest can stretch from early summer into autumn. To get the most from red raspberries, plant at least two kinds: a main-crop variety for heavy, early summer harvests and an autumn (or everbearing) type to close out the berry harvest. Bramble fruits are productive throughout all zones. The yield is 2 quarts (2 liters) per plant.

Cherries

Sweet cherries become medium to large trees. Tart cherries on a dwarf rootstock are scarcely larger than a bush, and because they're self-fertile, one is enough. The yield for sweet cherries is 30 quarts (31 liters), and for tart, 15 quarts (15.2 liters) (early summer). Cherries produce reliably through zone 5; tart or sour cherries through zone 4.

Grapes

Grapes on a trellis are good for masking a fence or for making a windbreak for vegetables or other tender plants. Traditionally, gardeners train the vines over arbors or trellises, but putting the vines so far overhead makes pruning and picking tough to do. The most-productive types of grapes yield up to 15 pounds (7 kg) per plant (late summer to early autumn). Grapes are productive through zone 3.

Peaches

Peaches can be tricky but are worth the effort. Peach trees get big, so put them where you'll enjoy their profile and glossy green foliage. Mulch to thwart grass and nourish trees. Where the climate is too cold for peaches (zone 5 and lower), consider sour cherries or apricots for this spot in the landscape. The yield is 3 to 5 bushels (105–175 liters) of peaches per tree (mid- to late summer).

Keeping pesky birds at bay

The pleasing sounds and movements that birds bring to your garden sometimes come at a cost. If you plan to grow fruits, you must take precautions to keep birds from devouring them. Birds especially love berries, and some eat corn and tomatoes. Effective deterrents include the following:

✔ **Polyester bird netting:** Sold at most garden centers, this barrier is by far the most reliable way to protect fruits and vegetables. Drape the netting over fruit-bearing plants as soon as fruits begin to ripen.

✔ **Birdscare flash tape:** This tape looks like metallic ribbon. Decorate the tops of plants with the stuff and trick birds into thinking the plant is on fire.

✔ **Fake predators:** These fool-the-eye figures include artificial snakes and owls, as well as good old scarecrows. Rearrange these phony spooks often to keep the birds baffled.

✔ **Noisemakers:** The devices include wind chimes, bells, rattling aluminum pie pans, and other items that make sounds when bumped by birds or jostled by the wind. Just use your imagination.

Pears

Pears are a bit easier to grow than apples. On dwarfing rootstock, pears reach 8 to 10 feet (2.4–3 m) tall. Train them as small pyramidal trees. Oriental pears, which are better adapted to the warmer regions, get one-third larger. You need two or more compatible varieties for pollination. The yield is 3 to 4 bushels (105–140 liters) per tree (late summer through autumn). Full-size pears produce reliably through zone 3; dwarf pear trees are hardy through zone 5.

Plums

Plums make nice small- to medium-size trees for a yard. Japanese and Japanese-American hybrids need cross-pollination by another variety from either group. Most European plums need another European pollinator; a few are self-fertile. The yield is 2 to 3 bushels (70–105 liters) (mid- to late summer). Plums regularly produce through zone 4.

Strawberries

Strawberries are the first fruits of the season, which may be why people treasure them so. An early and a late variety provide strawberries for two to three weeks. Grow them in 3- to 4-foot-wide (91–120 cm) beds and be ready to lay netting over the plants to keep out the birds. You need to renovate strawberry beds every two or three years. The yield is 1 quart (1 liter) per plant (late spring to early summer). Strawberries are hardy to all zones.

Chapter 7

Feed Me, Seymour! Watering, Feeding, and Composting

. . . .

In This Chapter

▶ Looking at the *why*s and *how*s of watering

▶ Understanding plant nutrients

▶ Fertilizing your plants

▶ Dabbling in the art and science of composting

. . . .

What's the most important thing you can do in your garden? The answer you get depends on whom you talk to and where that gardener lives. An Arizona gardener may say nothing is more important than watering (unless it's keeping roadrunners out of the barrel cactus collection). Someone with a lot of container plants will put fertilizing first. If you have horrid soil, nothing — we mean *nothing* — is more essential than composting.

So, what do we say? Our answer, of course, is . . . all of the above. But the amount of watering, feeding, and composting (the big three of your support system for healthy plant growth) you do depends on where you live, what you grow, and all sorts of other local conditions. But take our word for it — each of the three is extremely important.

Watering Basics

How much water your plants need to stay healthy depends on a number of factors:

- ✔ **Climate:** If you live in an area like Seattle, Washington, or Biloxi, Mississippi, where rainfall is regular and reliable, watering isn't a constant chore — except in prolonged dry spells or periods of drought. In drier areas like Los Angeles, watering is something that gardeners need to squeeze into their schedules almost on a daily basis.

- ✔ **Weather:** The average weather where you live on a season-to-season, year-to-year basis determines climate. Weather is what's happening outside right now. Out-of-the ordinary weather can wreak havoc on your plants. Hot, dry winds can fry plants even when the soil is moist.

- ✔ **Soil types:** Different soil types also affect how often a garden needs water.

   - **Sandy soil** holds water about as effectively as a sieve. Water penetrates sandy soils readily and deeply but tends to filter right on through. Adding organic matter — like compost, leaf mold, peat moss, or ground bark — helps sandy soils retain moisture.

   - **Heavy clay soil** is the exact opposite of sand — the dense particles in clay cause the soil to crust over and deflect water drops. Water applied slowly and in stages soaks in deeply; water applied quickly just runs off. Saturated clay holds water very well — sometimes so well that the plants rot. Adding plenty of organic matter helps break up the soil and improves drainage.

- ✔ **Location:** In general, shady gardens need less water than those receiving direct sun. However, in places where trees cast the shadows, their roots may greedily hog all the water, leaving little for the flowers. In such cases, applying enough water to satisfy both the trees and the flowers without causing disease or other problems may be almost impossible.

> ✔ **Genetic disposition:** Most plants need a consistent supply of moisture to remain healthy and free-blooming. Some types, however, can get by on less water than others.

Getting water to your garden

The best watering method for you may depend on how large a space you have. For example, with just a small bed of marigolds, you may find that watering with a handheld watering can or hose is not only effective but rewarding. If, however, you have a 200-square-foot (19 m²) mixed flower bed, watering effectively by hand is not only impractical, it is impossible.

In some areas, certain watering techniques become a matter of necessity instead of practicality. Where droughts are common or water supplies are unpredictable, conservation is the order of the day. You need to water in ways that hold every drop precious. Where foliage diseases like powdery mildew are common, you want to keep water off the plant leaves and apply the water only to the roots.

The following sections describe many fundamental watering methods.

Hand watering

If you want to stand among your heliotrope with a hose and water the plants by hand, that's fine. Hose-end attachments soften the force of the spray and help apply the water over a larger area. You can control the amount of water each plant gets and even do some pest control at the same time — blast that blanket flower to wash away aphids! Hand watering, however, takes time, especially in large gardens — and most of us aren't patient enough to stand and water the entire time it takes to supply enough water.

Sprinklers

Hose-end sprinklers come in a wide range of styles and sprinkler patterns. You've probably used a few of them. The problem with watering with sprinklers is that you have to drag the hose all around and move the sprinkler every so often. Also, most hose-end sprinklers don't apply water very evenly. If you forget to turn off the sprinkler, you waste a lot of water.

If you need help remembering to turn off the sprinklers, check out the various timers that are available. Some fit conveniently between the faucet and hose and so help prevent wasting water when watering the lawn.

One other possible problem with sprinkler watering is the wet foliage that results. In humid climates, overhead watering can spread disease and turn flowers into a moldy mess. On the other hand, in hot, dry climates, wetting the foliage rinses dust off the leaves, cools the plants, and helps prevent spider mite infestations.

Furrow irrigation

Furrows are shallow trenches that run parallel to your rows. Usually, you dig the furrows with a hoe at planting time and then plant a row of flowers or vegetables on either side of the furrow. Ideally, the bed should slope just the tiniest bit so that water runs naturally from one end of the furrow to the other (see Figure 7-1). When you want to water, you just put a slowly running hose at the end of the furrow and wait for the water to reach the other end.

Figure 7-1: Furrow irrigation uses gravity to carry water from one end of the furrow to the other.

Furrow irrigation, unlike sprinkler watering, keeps the foliage dry and doesn't promote disease. However, you do have to move the hose around frequently, and furrow watering doesn't work well on fast-draining, sandy soil. (The water soaks in too quickly and never reaches the other end of the furrow.)

Drip irrigation

Drip irrigation is a very effective and efficient way to water plants. Water slowly drips through tiny holes, or *emitters,* in black plastic pipe. The pipe connects to a water supply, a filter, and, often, a pressure regulator. The pipes weave among and around the plants, applying water directly to the base of the plants. You can either lay the pipe right on top of the soil and cover it with a mulch, or bury it a few inches deep. Most people like to keep the pipe close to the surface so that they can check it for clogs or fix breaks.

Drip emitters can wet an entire planting bed from one end to the other at each watering. (You can either snap the emitters into the pipe or buy the pipes with the emitters already installed.) Space the emitters 12 inches (30.5 cm) apart along the length of the pipe. Arrange the pipes so that you have no more than 18 inches (45 cm) between lengths or loops, as shown in Figure 7-2. The moisture radiates sideways and underground and wets the soil between emitters.

Figure 7-2: Drip irrigation is an efficient watering solution.

Drip systems usually have to run for at least several hours to wet a large area. Watch the soil carefully the first few times you water. Dig around to see how far the water has traveled over a given time and then make adjustments in how long you water in the future.

Most nurseries sell drip irrigation systems. You can also purchase them through the mail. Emitters are available with different application rates, varying by the number of gallons applied per hour. Pressure-compensating emitters apply water consistently from one end of the line to the other regardless of pressure changes due to uneven ground. Leaky pipe hoses, which are made of recycled tires, leak water along their entire length, but they apply water unevenly if the ground is not perfectly level.

If you live in an area where the soil freezes, to prevent bursting don't leave your drip system outside in winter. Instead, drain the water, roll up the tubing, and store it in the garage.

Automated watering systems

Automated watering systems can be real time-savers and can give you the freedom to safely take a vacation in the middle of summer. You can find an interesting mixture of timers at your local irrigation supplier or in mail-order catalogs. Some timers hook between hose bib and hose; others connect to valves and underground pipes that supply sprinklers. You can even build a moisture sensor into an automated system so that the water comes on only when the soil is dry. You can automate both drip and sprinkler systems.

Grass lawns have their own special water requirements as well as a world of irrigation methods.

Determining the amount and frequency of watering

A plant's water needs vary with the weather and the seasons. Even an automated system needs adjusting to water less in spring than in summer. You need to learn to be a pretty good observer and make adjustments accordingly.

Irrigation hardware is useless if you don't have a clue as to how much water your plants need. The answer is to water just enough, but not too much.

The best way to water is to replace the moisture the plants use up by watering daily, three times per week, or weekly. Plants lose moisture through their foliage because of *transpiration.* The soil also gives up water by *evaporation.* The combination of evaporation and transpiration is evapotranspiration.

Evapotranspiration, the combined loss of water from soil due to evaporation and transpiration through a plant's leaves, is one way to figure how much water you need to apply. Hot, dry, and windy weather causes plants to use much more moisture than they do on a cool, overcast day. The *evapotranspiration rate,* measured as the total number of inches of water per week or month, tells how much water you can add to replace what the soil lost and what the plants used. Using the evapotranspiration rate is a more accurate way to judge how much to water than the old-fashioned, and often inaccurate, "1 inch (2.5 cm) per week" general rule.

If you live in regions where irrigation is a fact of life, the local newspaper (usually on the page with the weather report) gives the recommended watering rate for lawns based on the evapotranspiration rate. If your local newspaper doesn't include such information, check with your local cooperative extension service.

To figure out how long you need to run the sprinklers to deliver a particular amount of water (usually expressed as inches of water), place containers in important locations throughout your sprinkler's spray pattern. Be sure the containers have straight, vertical sides — juice cans work well. Run the sprinkler for a specific length of time, such as one hour. With a metal ruler, measure the depth of water in each can. Use the can with the least amount of water as the standard (hopefully, it's not too different from the others), because even the area that receives the least must get enough.

Now you can water by the newspaper's guideline. If, for example, the sprinkler test shows that your sprinkler puts out ¾ inch (2 cm) per hour and the paper says to apply 1½ inches (about 4 cm) of water this week, run your sprinkler for two hours. This same rate is a good starting point for trees, shrubs, annual flowers, and vegetables.

However, you can use other ways to tell when your plants need water:

✔ **Note the condition of your plants.** When plants start to dry out, the leaves get droopy and wilt. The plant may also lose its bright green color and start to look a little drab. Now, your goal is to water before a plant gets to that point, but the plant will show you when it needs water more often.

✔ **Dig in the ground.** Most plants need water when the top 2 to 3 inches (5–7.5 cm) of soil is dry. So take a small trowel or shovel and dig around a bit. If the top of the soil is dry, you need to water.

Eventually, through observation and digging, you start to develop a watering schedule, and a lot of the guesswork disappears.

Conserving water

Water shortages are a reality in almost any climate or region. Following are a few things you can do when water is scarce or limited, when you want to reduce your water bill, or when you just want to conserve the precious resource of fresh water.

✔ **Use a timer.** Don't tell us you've never forgotten to turn the water off and flooded half the neighborhood. Just set an egg timer or an alarm clock to let you know when it's time to shut off the water. Or get even more high-tech and use one of the automated timers mentioned in this chapter.

✔ **Install drip irrigation.** This watering method applies water slowly without runoff. Drip is definitely the most frugal watering system you can use.

✔ **Mulch, mulch, and mulch some more.** Several inches of compost, shredded fir bark, leaf mold, or other material cools the soil and reduces evaporation, thus saving water. And as the mulch breaks down, it improves the soil. For more on mulches, see Chapter 4.

✔ **Pull weeds.** Weeds steal water meant for your plants. Pull out weeds regularly. For more on weeds, see Chapter 9.

✔ **Water deeply and infrequently.** Shallow sprinkling does very little good. Water to a depth of 8 to 10 inches (20–25 cm), then let the soil dry out partially before you water again. This method encourages plants to develop deep roots, which can endure longer periods between waterings.

✔ **Water early.** Water early in the day when temps are cooler and it's less windy. That way, less water evaporates into the air and more reaches the roots.

✔ **Use rainwater.** Put a barrel or other collector where the drain pipes from your roof empty out. Then use that water on your garden.

✔ **Measure rainfall.** Keep track of how much rain you get. An inch is usually enough to let you skip a watering.

✔ **Plant at the right time.** Plant when your plants have the best chance of getting fully established, before the onset of very hot or very cold weather.

Providing a Balanced Diet for Your Plants

Before you head for the nursery to pick up a bag of fertilizer, remember that understanding the nutrients that plants need and how plants use them is helpful.

Sixteen elements are known to be essential for healthy plant growth. Plants particularly need carbon, hydrogen, and oxygen in large quantities. Plants also need energy from sunlight for *photosynthesis,* the process by which green plants take carbon dioxide from the air and water from the soil to produce sugars to fuel their growth. Apart from watering plants, gardeners can trust nature to supply these big basic requirements.

Plants also need nitrogen, phosphorus, and potassium in relatively large quantities. These three elements are often called *macronutrients,* or *primary nutrients.* Plants take up these three nutrients from the soil. If they are not present in the soil, you can supply them by adding fertilizers. The percentages of these nutrients are the three prominent numbers on any bag or box of fertilizer, and the nutrients always appear in the same order. For more on fertilizer, see this chapter's section "Don't Compromise, Fertilize!"

- ✔ **Nitrogen (N):** This nutrient, represented by the chemical symbol N, is responsible for the healthy green color of your plants. It is a key part of proteins and *chlorophyll,* the plant pigment that plays a vital role in photosynthesis. Plants with a nitrogen deficiency show a yellowing of older leaves first, along with a general slowdown in growth.

- ✔ **Phosphorus (P):** Phosphorus is associated with good root growth, increased disease resistance, and fruit and seed formation. Plants lacking in phosphorus are stunted and have dark green foliage, followed by reddening of the stems and leaves. As with nitrogen, the symptoms appear on the older leaves first.

- ✔ **Potassium (K):** This nutrient promotes vigorous growth and disease resistance. The first sign of a deficiency shows up as browning of the edges of leaves. Older leaves become affected first.

- ✔ **Calcium, magnesium, and sulfur:** Plants need these three *secondary nutrients* in substantial quantities but not to the same extent as nitrogen, phosphorus, and potassium. Where the soil is acid (areas of high rainfall), calcium and magnesium are important to add to acidify the soil. Doing so maintains a soil pH beneficial to plants and supplies the nutrient that the plants need. Where the soil is alkaline (areas of low rainfall), adding sulfur to the soil is similarly beneficial. For more about pH, see Chapter 4.

- ✔ **Iron, manganese, copper, boron, molybdenum, chlorine, and zinc:** These seven elements are the *micronutrients,* meaning plants need only minute quantities for good health. These nutrients are often not lacking in the soil, but they may be unavailable to plant roots. The cause of this problem is usually a soil pH that is too acid or too alkaline. In this case, rather than adding the nutrient, adjusting soil pH is the remedy. Too much of any of these nutrients can be harmful.

Don't Compromise, Fertilize!

After you decide to feed your plants, you'll face a myriad of fertilizers at the nursery. How do you know which kinds to buy?

When you buy a commercial fertilizer, its analysis appears on the label with three numbers. These three numbers are helpful because they let you know the amounts of nutrients (N-P-K) that are in a particular fertilizer.

- The first number indicates the percentage of nitrogen (N).
- The second number, the percentage of phosphorus (P_2O_5).
- The third, the percentage of potassium (K_2O).

A 100-pound (43 kg) bag of 5-10-10 fertilizer consists of 5 percent nitrogen (5 pounds/2.3 kg), 10 percent phosphate (10 pounds/4.6 kg), and 10 percent potash (10 pounds/4.6 kg). Altogether, the bag has 25 pounds of plant-usable nutrients. The remaining 75 pounds (34 kg) usually consists of only *carrier,* or filler; a small amount of the filler may contain some plant-usable nutrients.

Any fertilizer that contains all three of the primary nutrients — N-P-K — is a *complete fertilizer.* The garden term *complete* has its basis in laws and regulations that apply to the fertilizer industry: It does not mean that the fertilizer literally contains everything a plant may need.

Common fertilizer terms

You don't need a degree in botany to have a lovely garden. But when looking for the right fertilizers, you do need to understand some of the terminology.

Take a look at some of the fertilizing terms you may encounter:

✔ **Chelated micronutrients:** The word *chelate* comes from the Latin word for *claw,* and that's a useful way to understand how these micronutrients function. These compounds bind to certain plant nutrients and essentially deliver them to the plant roots. Nutrients that plants require in minute quantities — such as iron, zinc, and manganese — are often available in chelated form. The chelated fertilizer you buy may be a powder or liquid.

✔ **Foliar:** As the name implies, foliar fertilizers are liquids that you apply on a plant's leaves. These fertilizers contain nutrients that plant leaves can absorb directly. Although a plant's roots also can absorb the nutrients in most foliar fertilizers, those absorbed via leaves have a quick effect. Don't apply foliar fertilizers in hot weather because leaves can become damaged.

✔ **Granular:** These fertilizers are the most common and most often sold in boxes or bags. Most granular fertilizers are partially soluble. For example, a 10-10-10 granular fertilizer is best applied to the soil about a month prior to planting in order for the nutrients to be available at planting time. You also can get special formulations, such as rose food or azalea food. These specialized fertilizers supply nutrients over a longer period of time than liquid or soluble fertilizers but not as long as slow-release kinds. (See Figure 7-3.)

Figure 7-3: Use a spreader to apply granular fertilizer.

✔ **Liquid:** Most kinds of fertilizers are dry, but some come as liquid in bottles and jugs. On a per-nutrient basis, liquid fertilizers are more expensive than most dry fertilizers. Most liquid fertilizers need further dilution in water, but a few are ready-to-use. Liquid fertilizers are easy to inject into irrigation systems, which is the reason many professional growers prefer them. (See Figure 7-4.)

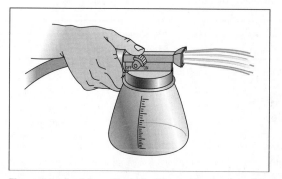

Figure 7-4: Applying a liquid fertilizer with a hose-end sprayer.

✔ **Organic:** These fertilizers are often made from dead or composted plants and animals. Examples are blood meal, fish emulsion, and manure. Usually, organic fertilizers contain significant amounts of only one of the major nutrients; for example, bone meal contains only phosphorus. Nutrients in organic fertilizers are made available to plant roots after soil microorganisms break down the nutrients. Activity of these microorganisms is fastest in summer when soils are warm. As a general rule, half the nutrients in organic fertilizers are available to plants the first season.

✔ **Slow-release:** These fertilizers release the nutrients they contain at specific rates in specific conditions over an extended period. For example, Osmocote fertilizers release nutrients in response to soil moisture. The nutrients inside the tiny beads "osmose" through a resin membrane. Soil microorganisms slowly act on another type — sulfur-coated urea — until the nutrients release. Some fertilizers can release their nutrients for as long as eight months. Slow-release fertilizers are very useful for container plants that otherwise need frequent fertilizing.

Kinds of fertilizers for various plants

Different kinds of plants need different kinds of fertilizers, and Table 7-1 lists our recommendations. Of course, the best advice before using any fertilizer is to have your soil tested. For more about soil testing, see Chapter 4.

Table 7-1	Fertilizing at a Glance	
Plant	*Fertilizer*	*Comments*
Annuals	Granular	Apply before planting, supplemented by liquid-soluble applications after planting.
Bulbs	Granular 8-8-8 or similar	Apply at planting time.
Fruit trees	Granular and/or organic	Apply as necessary in spring only.
Hanging baskets	Slow-release or liquid soluble	Apply every two weeks.
House plants	Slow-release or liquid soluble	
Lawns	Granular and/or organic 28-7-14 or similar, preferably slow-release; or an organic, high-nitrogen fertilizer	
Perennials	Granular and/or organic	Apply in autumn; supplement with liquid-soluble.
Roses	Granular and/or organic	Apply in spring and autumn for good growth.
Trees and shrubs	Granular and/or organic	Apply in autumn; supplement with complete granular (10-10-10 or similar) if spring growth is poor.

Plant	Fertilizer	Comments
Vegetables	Organic	Apply in autumn or at least one month prior to planting. Continually enrich soil with organic fertilizers; supplement with granular 5-10-10 first two gardening seasons.

Organic fertilizers

Organic or natural fertilizers such as manure and composts are more cumbersome and possibly more expensive than synthetic fertilizers, but nothing quite takes their place. These fertilizers provide some nutrient value and, when you incorporate them into the soil, improve soil structure, which increases the soil's ability to hold air, nutrients, and water.

Plants take up nutrients in specific forms, regardless of whether the source is organic or synthetic. You can supply all the nutrients that plants need by using only organic materials, but you need to use some care and effort to ensure that sufficient amounts of nitrogen, phosphorus, and potash are available to the plants throughout the season.

Because the nutrients in organic materials are tied up in more complex molecules, these nutrients often take longer to become available to the plants, which can result in temporary nutrient deficiencies, especially in the spring.

Fresh manure can "burn" plants (damaging leaves and growth from excess application) just as surely as any chemical fertilizer, whereas woody materials (wood chips, sawdust, leaf piles, and so on) can cause a temporary nitrogen deficiency until they are sufficiently decomposed. The microorganisms that help the decay process may use up all the available nitrogen to break down the woody material. You can counteract this effect somewhat by applying a little extra nitrogen in the spring. A rule of green thumb is that when the material starts to resemble soil, it is ready for the garden.

Piling Onto the Compost Bandwagon

As we visit the gardens of friends and neighbors around the country, a stop at the compost pile is a must in almost every garden tour. Meeting a gardener who shows off a rich, dark, earthy compost as eagerly as towering dahlias is not at all unusual.

Not so long ago, we gardeners hid our compost piles. In privacy, we would witness the magic of composting, the transformation of garden and yard waste into sweet-smelling black gold. We feared that others (especially neighbors) would judge our passion as a waste of time and space.

Attitudes have changed. Landfills are filling up, and some states even ban yard waste from landfills. Composting is now widely recognized as an easy, effective way to reduce solid waste at home.

More to the heart of gardeners is the fact that compost is a valuable, natural soil amendment. Adding compost to garden beds and planting holes enhances nutrients and improves soil texture. Compost helps loosen heavy clay soils, and it increases the water-holding capacity of sandy soils. (See Chapter 4 for more about soils.)

A *compost pile* is a collection of plant (and sometimes animal) materials, combined in a way to encourage quick decomposition. Soil microorganisms (bacteria and fungi) do the work of breaking down this organic material into a soil-like consistency.

These organisms need oxygen and water to survive. Turning the pile over provides oxygen, and an occasional watering helps keep it moist. If the pile is well-made and the organisms are thriving, it heats up quickly and doesn't emit any unpleasant odors. Finished compost that looks and feels like dark, crumbly soil can, thus, take as little as a month to produce.

From refuse to riches

Whether you make your compost in an elaborate store-bought bin (one that closes tightly) or simply in a freestanding pile, the essentials of good composting are the same. To get fast results, follow these steps:

1. **Collect equal parts, by volume, of dried, brown, carbon-rich material (like old leaves or straw) and fresh, green, nitrogen-rich material (fresh-cut grass, green vegetation, and vegetable kitchen wastes).**

   A few materials should *not* be used in an open compost pile. Although farm animal manures are a safe source of nitrogen for the pile, dog and cat waste can spread unhealthy organisms. Meat, fats, bones, and cooked foods decompose slowly, may be smelly, and may attract animal pests — add these only to compost bins that close tightly. Avoid chemically treated lawn clippings and diseased plant material. Finally, keep out tenacious weeds that spread by runners and roots, such as Bermuda grass.

2. **Chop or shred the organic materials into small pieces, if possible.**

   Pieces that are ¾ inch (2 cm) or smaller are ideal because they break down quickly.

3. **Build the pile at least 3 feet by 3 feet by 3 feet (1 cubic yard or 1 m³), alternating layers of the carbon-rich material with the green material.**

   Layer a thin covering of soil for every 18 inches of depth. The soil carries more microorganisms that aid in decomposition.

4. **Wet the pile as you build it.**

   Keep the material moist, not soaked. (It should be about as moist as a wrung-out sponge.)

5. **After the temperature begins to decrease, turn the pile, wetting it as necessary to keep it moist.**

   A well-built pile heats up in approximately a week, peaking between 120°F and 160°F (49°C to 71°C). If you don't have a compost thermometer, use a garden fork to turn the pile every week or so the first month.

Bin there, done that!

A compost pile cares not whether it's caged or freestanding. An enclosure, called a *compost bin* (see Figure 7-5), mostly keeps the pile neat and can help retain moisture and heat. Depending on its design, a compost bin also keeps out animal pests. For these reasons, especially in urban settings, a bin is a good idea.

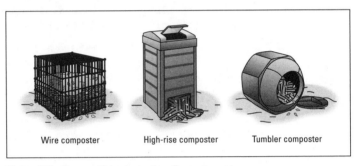

Wire composter High-rise composter Tumbler composter

Figure 7-5: Compost bins keep the pile neat.

To build or to buy?

Bins are available by mail order and, increasingly, through nurseries, garden centers, and even discount stores. You can spend up to $400 or more for a commercial compost bin, or you can make your own with scrap materials.

A *wire bin* is perhaps the easiest type to make. You need an 11-foot (3.5 m) length of 36-inch-wide (1 m), welded reinforcing wire with a grid of about 2 x 4 inches (5 x 10 cm). Simply bend the wire to form a hoop and tie the ends together with strong wire. Lining the wire mesh with landscape fabric helps prevent the pile from drying out excessively. This bin holds about a cubic yard when full.

To use the bin, fill it with the appropriate balance of organic material. When the pile is ready to turn, lift off the wire mesh and set it next to the pile; then, turn the material and fork it back into the enclosure.

Another option is a *wooden compost bin,* made with wooden pallets, wooden scrap boards, and wire or — for the more elaborate model — 2 x 4 (5 x 10 cm) and 2 x 6 (5 x 15 cm) lumber. The Cadillac of the wooden compost bins uses three bins arranged side by side, as shown in Figure 7-6. Though this bin can be time-consuming to construct, some gardeners prefer the convenience of a three-box bin. Each bin is for compost at a different stage of maturity. For example, fresh material is added to the far-left bin, turned into the middle one after a few weeks, and then turned into the bin at the far right to finish.

Figure 7-6: A wooden compost bin with three bins allows for easy turning.

Commercial bins come in four basic flavors:

✔ **Containers for hot compost:** Usually made out of recycled plastic, these bottomless boxes or cylinders are designed to be used in much the same way as the wire bin. You completely fill the bin with the right blend of materials and let the pile heat up. To turn the compost, when the bin is full, you lift off the top section of compost and place it on the ground (the section on top now becomes the section on the bottom). Then you reach in with a fork and lift some of the lower compost, making it the top section of compost, and so on.

Some of these containers are stackable, which makes removing them and turning the compost easier. With sufficient turning, this type of bin delivers fast results.

✔ **Bins for a static pile:** With these plastic units (which usually have air vents along the sides), you make a compost pile by putting a balance of waste materials in the top of the bin and letting the mixture sit. As the waste decomposes, you remove the finished compost from the bottom of the bin and add more waste to the top.

This type of bin is the most commonly available bin, although not necessarily the best. You don't need to do any turning, and you can add waste at any time; however, decomposition is slow, and you get only small amounts of compost at a time. Because the pile does not get very hot, weeds, seeds, and plant diseases may survive.

✔ **Tumblers:** With a tumbler, you place your compost inside the container and then turn the entire bin to toss the compost inside. Some tumblers have crank handles for turning. One tumbler system is designed to roll on the ground, tumbling the compost inside as it goes.

With these units, you make a hot compost by balancing the waste materials and turning the bin frequently. Tumblers are generally the most expensive type of bin, but the ease of turning and the fast results may be worth the money. Choose one with at least a 1-cubic-yard (1 m³) capacity and test it for ease of loading and turning before you buy.

✔ **Anaerobic containers:** These sealed, closed-to-air compost bins require no turning or aerating. You simply fill the container with organic material, close the lid, and wait, sometimes up to six months.

Although no maintenance is required, this type of bin often has insect and odor problems. The decomposed product is slimy and requires drying before use, and shoveling the compost out of the bin is difficult. We give this product low marks for home gardeners.

Composting aids . . . who needs them?

You don't need to have any store-bought gadgets to make compost. With or without accessories, you can create a perfect pile. A few supplies, however, do make composting faster, more exacting, and perhaps easier. The following is a rundown of these handy items for your consideration. All are available through mail-order garden supply catalogs.

✔ **Compost starter:** Manufacturers say these products, sometimes called *inoculants* or *activators,* accelerate the composting process and improve the quality of the finished compost. We say you don't really need them, and that adding a little garden soil for every 12- to 18-inch (30–46 cm) layer of yard waste will accomplish the same thing. At most you might want to add a little cotton or soybean meal, but only then if the materials are mostly brown (high in carbon).

As an alternative to buying a commercial starter, make a thin layer of rich garden soil when you first build your pile.

✔ **Compost thermometer:** This thermometer consists of a face dial and a steel probe (about 20 inches/50 cm long). You use this tool to accurately monitor the temperature of compost. The instrument measures temperatures from 0°F to 220°F (–18°C to 104°C) and enables you to know when your pile is cooking and when it is cooling down and ready to turn. After you insert the steel probe into the pile, you can see the temperature reading on the face dial. If the compost gets hot, meaning up to 140°F to 160°F (60°C to 71°C), most of the bad players — weeds, diseases, and insect eggs — get killed.

✔ **Compost aerating tool:** You push a galvanized steel tool, which is about 36 inches (1 m) long, into the compost pile. As you pull the tool out, two paddles open, creating a churning action that enables oxygen to enter the pile.

✔ **Compost sifter:** Because different materials decompose at different rates, you may end up with some large chunks of not-yet-decomposed material in compost that is otherwise ready for the garden. The sifter separates out the large pieces, which you can then toss back into a new compost pile to further decompose.

You can save a few bucks by making your own sifter. To do so, use ¼-inch (0.5 cm) window screen stapled or nailed to a wooden frame made of lumber. Make the frame large enough so that you can position it over a wheelbarrow and sift compost through it.

✔ **Pitchfork:** This long-handled tool, with tines about 10 to 12 inches (25–30 cm) long, is the best instrument to use for turning compost.

Heapin' it on

So what else can you put in your compost pile besides the obvious? The following list describes several other materials found around the home and garden that make good additions to any compost pile:

✔ Ashes from the wood stove (sprinkle them lightly between layers; *don't* add them by the bucketful)

✔ Chicken or rabbit manure

✔ Coffee grounds and tea leaves

✔ Eggshells (crush them before adding)

✔ Flowers

✔ Fruit and vegetable peels, stalks, and foliage (everything from salad leftovers to old pea vines)

✔ Fruit pulp from a juicer

✔ Grass clippings (mix them thoroughly to prevent clumping)

✔ Hedge clippings

✔ Shredded leaves (whole leaves tend to mat down and block air)

✔ Pine needles (use sparingly; they break down slowly)

✔ Sawdust

✔ Sod and soil

✔ Wood chips (chipped very small for faster decomposition)

Homemade compost tea

Compost tea is a genetic cocktail teeming with microorganisms that appear to boost a plant's natural defenses and suppress the growth of some fungi. It can help reduce the spread of botrytis molds, tomato early and late blights, downy mildew, and powdery mildew by 50 to 90 percent. Make the tea by mixing one part mature compost that contains some manure with five parts water in a bucket. Let the mixture sit in the shade for about ten days. Then filter the solution through cheesecloth, dilute the tea to half strength if you want, and spray it or dribble it on the leaves. Try to coat both sides. Reapply after two to three weeks. You can also spread the leftover residue on the ground around your plants. Avoid spraying any products containing manures directly on leafy vegetables such as lettuce and spinach that you'll soon be harvesting.

Warning: When you use any disease-control remedies on food crops, be sure to wash your harvest well before eating it.

Chapter 8

Fighting Pests and Diseases

In This Chapter

▶ Dealing with pesky insects

▶ Controlling common garden pests

▶ Keeping beneficial insects happy

▶ Curing plant diseases

*T*he key to a healthy garden may sound a bit strange to you, but here it is: Don't sweat the small stuff. The more you try for a perfect, pest-free garden, the more likely you are to invite problems. Not only is accepting a certain amount of damage realistic, it also makes gardening more fun and less frustrating. Don't try to vanquish all enemies and leave them decimated, but do try to outsmart them, perhaps losing a battle but winning the war.

In addition, when you discover more about pests and diseases — and the conditions that invite them — you arm yourself with new techniques to reduce damage while promoting a healthier garden. This chapter gives you a start in that direction.

Insect Pests You're Most Likely to Encounter

Do borers drive you buggy? Don't know the difference between a cutworm and a caterpillar? In this section, we describe common North American pests and give you some tips on how to deal with them.

Aphids

These tiny, soft-bodied, pear-shaped pests (shown in Figure 8-1) suck plant sap with their needlelike noses. Colors vary: They may be black, green, red, or even translucent. Aphids leave behind sticky sap droppings that may turn black if covered with sooty mold. Aphids can proliferate quickly on weakened plants. Blast them off with a hose, control with beneficial insects or sticky yellow traps, or spray with insecticidal soap. The beneficial insects green lacewings and ladybird beetles are also excellent controls.

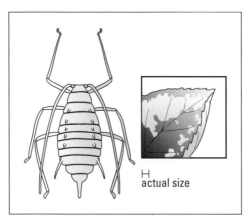

actual size

Figure 8-1: Aphids proliferate quickly on weakened plants.

Apple maggots

Slightly smaller than houseflies, these pests overwinter in soil, then appear beginning in June or July to begin laying eggs in apples, crabapples, plums, and other fruits. Mostly a problem for northern gardeners. Always dispose of infested fruit before maggots emerge and establish in the soil. Trap adult flies by hanging red, apple-shaped spheres coated with sticky goo. Begin trapping by early July and continue through August, cleaning and refreshing the sticky stuff every two weeks. Bait traps with butyl hexanoate pheromone.

Instead of coating the red trap itself with the sticky stuff, enclose the trap in a small plastic bag and cover the bag with the trapping material. To renew the trap, dispose of the old plastic bag and replace with a new one.

An improvement on the red sphere trap is the Ladd trap, a red sphere bisected with a yellow sheet.

Bean leaf beetles

These small, orange-red beetles have black heads and black spots and are about the size of a ladybird beetle. The beetles feed on leaves, creating a lacy pattern. Cover seedlings with lightweight row covers to exclude exploring beetles. To reduce damage caused by an existing infestation, spray with neem or insecticidal soap.

Black vine weevils

This dark, crawling, 1- to 2-inch-long (2.5–5 cm) beetle chews on the foliage of evergreen trees and shrubs such as rhododendrons and yews, while the larvae attack from the other end, eating the roots. Black vine weevils also attack potted plants. Control adults and larvae with beneficial nematodes.

Borers

Several kinds of beetle and caterpillar larvae (they look like small worms and are usually less than 1 inch/2.5 cm long) tunnel into the wood or stems of fruit trees, white birches, dogwoods, shade trees, rhododendrons, German irises, and squash vines. The boring weakens the plant and makes it more susceptible to diseases. The holes can also cut off nutrient flow to the affected limb or vine. Choose species that are less susceptible to borers. For example, try Siberian irises instead of German bearded irises. Keep susceptible plants growing vigorously and watch for signs of borer damage — dead bark, sawdust piles, and poor performance. When you find borers, cut off and destroy severely infested limbs. Inject parasitic nematodes into the remaining borer holes.

Caterpillars

Moth and butterfly larvae are avid eaters that can cause damage to a variety of plants. However, you may decide to overlook the activities of some butterfly caterpillars so that you can enjoy the handsome butterflies later. Eliminate caterpillars such as the cabbage looper, tomato hornworm, and corn earworm before they do too much damage. If beneficial insects don't keep them in check, spray with Bt.

Chinch bugs

These ¼-inch-long (0.6 cm), brown or black insects suck grass sap, releasing toxins that make grass discolor and wilt. They can turn entire patches of lawn brown, especially in dry and hot areas. They are especially a problem on St. Augustine grass in southern areas. Dethatch the lawn and let it grow a little longer than usual to discourage chinch bugs. For control, treat with a neem insecticide.

Codling moths

These 1-inch-long (2.5 cm), pinkish-white caterpillars emerge from eggs laid on apples, peaches, pears, and other fruits. The adult moth is about ½ inch (1.2 cm) long and brown. The caterpillars tunnel inside the fruit, usually ruining it. In early spring, while the tree is still dormant and leafless, spray dormant oil to kill overwintering eggs. Right after flowering, use pheromone traps to trap egg-laying females. Spray with Bt when apples are about ½-inch (1.2 cm) in diameter, or spray with neem as needed to prevent egg-laying through the growing season. Eliminate wild or unsprayed trees nearby that shelter codling moth populations.

Pheromones are the perfumes of the insect world. Undetectable to us, female butterflies and moths release tiny amounts of these chemicals, which are a siren song to a wandering male of the right type. Professionals use synthetic pheromones to monitor pest populations; you can use them to trap and disorient codling moth.

Hang traps at eye level and spray Bt or neem oil three or four times beginning a week to ten days after beginning of petal fall, or after the first codling moth is trapped.

Colorado potato beetles

This yellow-and-black-striped beetle — ⅓ inch (0.8 cm) long, and nearly round — is notorious for obliterating potato plantings, but it also eats tomatoes, eggplants, petunias, and flowering tobacco. Discourage Colorado potato beetles by rotating planting sites. Cover potato plants with floating row covers to keep the beetles off. Spray with Bt formulated for Colorado potato beetles, or use neem. Beneficial nematodes also destroy larvae in soil.

Corn earworms

These annoying caterpillars feed right at the tips of ears of corn. They'll chew right through silk to get to kernels, and sometimes eat leaves. A daub of mineral oil on the developing silk prevents most damage. You can also spray Bt and rely on the help of beneficial trichogramma wasps that parasitize the worms. See "Encouraging 'good' insects," later in this chapter, for more about trichogramma wasps.

Cucumber beetles

These ⅓-inch-long (0.8 cm) beetles with yellow and black stripes (or spots) swarm on cucumber, squash, and melon plants. You're likely to spot them first crawling around inside flowers. The main threat they pose is a bacterial wilt disease they carry that will kill your plants. That disease is reason enough to keep the beetles away entirely. Cover young vines with floating row covers. Uncover when several flowers open, and spray as needed with pyrethrin or dust with *diatomaceous earth* (see the "Safe and effective pest chemicals" section, later in this chapter). Till the soil in autumn to eliminate over-wintering hideouts.

Curculios

These ¼-inch-long (0.6 cm) beetles are easy to identify by the crescent-shaped, egg-laying cut they make in fruit. Unfortunately, after the beetles lay the eggs, the fruit may be ruined. Spread out a tarp or old sheet underneath the tree, shake apple and pear tree branches to knock the beetles off, and then step on them. Also destroy prematurely fallen fruit, which may contain larvae. If the problem is severe, consider spraying the insecticide *imidan.* Experts recommend the insecticide as the safest and most effective of available sprays.

Cutworms

These ½-inch-long (1.2 cm), grayish caterpillars emerge on spring and early summer nights to eat the base of young seedling stems, cutting the tops off from the roots, as shown in Figure 8-2. To control, surround seedlings with a barrier that prevents the cutworms from crawling close and feeding. These devices can be as simple as an empty cardboard toilet paper roll or a collar made from aluminum foil — just make sure that the collar encircles the stem completely and set 1 inch (2.5 cm) deep in the soil.

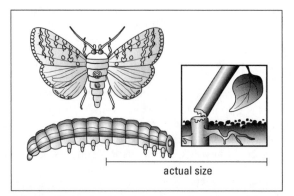

actual size

Figure 8-2: Cutworms can do a great deal of damage before sprouting wings and flying off.

Flea beetles

These tiny black beetles feed on vegetable plants such as egg-plant, radish, and broccoli, sometimes riddling the entire leafy area of seedlings with tiny holes. Cover susceptible plants with floating row covers as soon as you plant them. Keep them covered until the plants get fairly large and can with-stand a few beetle bites. You also can spray with neem.

Gypsy moths

These 2-inch-long (5 cm), gray (with brown hairs), foliage-eating caterpillars or their egg clusters hitchhike across the country on cars, campers, and trains. They eat foliage on a number of shade trees, including oaks, and can defoliate trees when their population gets large enough. Monitor population sizes with pheromone traps. Catch caterpillars as they attempt to crawl up tree trunks by using duct tape treated with a sticky barrier. Spray with Bt or neem.

Sticky pest barriers are just that — bands of goop that a crawling insect cannot navigate. Buy this stuff at garden centers or from a mail-order supplier.

Japanese beetles

These beetles (pictured in Figure 8-3) are ½ inch (1.2 cm) long, and are metallic blue-green with coppery wing covers. They eat almost any plant with gusto. Their fat, white, C-shaped, ¾-inch-long (2 cm) larvae consume turf roots. To control, treat your lawn with milky spore disease, which takes several years to spread through the lawn, or with parasitic nematodes, a quicker-acting helper. Inspect your garden in the evening or after dark for the beetles, knocking them off plants into a can or bucket of soapy water. You can also spray with neem.

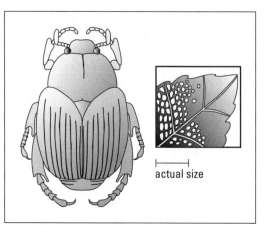

actual size

Figure 8-3: Japanese beetles consume almost any plant.

Avoid using the Japanese beetle traps that you can hang. The pheromones in these traps attract beetles not only from your yard, but from your neighbors' yards as well. You'll end up with more beetles than you would have had without the traps.

Aliens invade!

The speed and convenience of modern travel and mail has been a boon to insects and diseases, too. That's how pests — such as the Asian longhorn beetle, gypsy moth, Japanese beetle, Mediterranean fruit fly, and silverleaf whitefly — got to North America. Historically, the spread of pests has been blocked by geography. Not so anymore. In the United States, the 1,800 inspectors and 62 canine teams (the "beagle brigade" of international airport fame) of the Animal and Plant Health Inspection Service (APHIS) lead the defense. Do farmers and fellow gardeners a favor and don't mail fruits home from foreign locations, and follow U.S. Customs and APHIS regulations when traveling overseas. If you intend to bring plants home, call APHIS first at 301-734-8645. To find out more about APHIS and U.S. Customs regulations, go to www.aphis.usda.gov and www.customs.ustreas.gov.

Leaf miners

The larval form of tiny flies, these maggots tunnel randomly through leaves of plants such as columbine, peppers, beans, and lilacs. They disfigure plants and are hard to eliminate because they're protected inside the leaf. Prevent infestation by covering predisposed seedlings with floating row covers and removing and destroying infested leaves. Spray with neem in spring when adults begin to lay eggs.

Mealybugs

These small sucking insects cover their bodies with a white, cottony substance that makes them easy to identify. Plus, they usually feed in groups. Mealybugs are common on house-plants. You can wash off small numbers with cotton dipped in rubbing alcohol. Spray indoor plants with an oil-based "leaf shine" product, and use horticultural oil for landscape plants. Insecticidal soap and neem are also effective remedies.

Mexican bean beetles

These ¼-inch (0.6 cm), round beetles are yellowish with black spots. They resemble ladybugs but are avid plant eaters. They can destroy an entire bean planting, enjoying snap beans most but also lima beans, soybeans, and other legumes. The spiny, yellow larvae that appear on the bean plants soon after the adults arrive are just as bad as the adults. Pull up and destroy infested plants, beetles and all, immediately after harvesting. Till the ground to kill beetles hiding there. If necessary, spray with soap, pyrethrin, horticultural oil, or neem.

Oriental fruit moths

These small moths produce ½-inch-long (1.2 cm), white-to-pink larvae that tunnel into the young wood or fruit of fruit and ornamental trees. In spring, work the soil shallowly around infested trees to kill overwintering larvae. Catch adult males in pheromone traps or use pheromones to confuse males and prevent breeding. You can kill moth eggs with horti-cultural oil.

Root maggots

These are a variety of fly larvae — most are white and less than ¼ inch long (0.6 cm) — that attack the roots of carrots, the cabbage family, and onions. They can disfigure or destroy these plants. Look for resistant plants. Cover new plantings of susceptible types of cabbage, turnips, rutabagas, radishes, kohlrabi, carrots, parsnips, and onions with floating row covers.

Scale

Looking like bumps on plant stems and leaves, these tiny sucking insects cling to plant branches, hiding under an outer shell that serves as a shield. These pests suck plant sap and can kill plants if present in large numbers. Look for sticky, honeylike sap droppings, one clue that scale may be present. Remove and destroy badly infested stems. Indoors or on small plants, clean off light infestations with a cotton ball soaked in rubbing alcohol. Spray larger plants with horticultural oil in early spring or summer.

Snails and slugs

These soft-bodied mollusks (see Figure 8-4) feed on tender leaves during the cool of night or in rainy weather. Sometimes they're hard to spot: All you see is the slime trail they leave behind. They proliferate in damp areas, hiding and breeding under rocks, mulch, and other garden debris. Clean up dark, damp hiding spots to relocate slugs elsewhere. Catch the ones that remain by setting a saucer with the rim at ground level. Fill the saucer with beer. Slugs crawl in and can't get out. Refill regularly. Or surround plants with copper barriers — metal strips that seem to shock slugs if they attempt to crawl across. Set out traps, commercial or homemade. Look for new, nontoxic baits that contain iron phosphate.

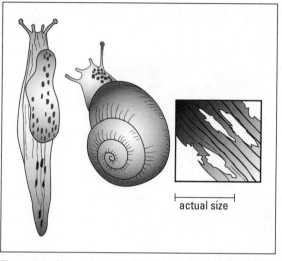

Figure 8-4: Slugs and snails like to live in cool, damp areas.

Make your own slug trap by placing a few boards or a rolled-up newspaper in the garden. In the early morning, lift the board and destroy the slugs. Toss out the newspaper if it has slugs.

Spider mites

These tiny arachnoids (shown greatly enlarged in Figure 8-5) are almost microscopic, but when they appear in large numbers, you can begin to see the fine webs that they weave. They suck plant sap, causing leaves to discolor and plants to lose vigor. They are especially active in arid conditions. You find spider mites on fruit trees, miniature roses, potted begonias, and many houseplants. Indoors, wash houseplants often and spray with insecticidal soap. Outdoors, wash plants with a strong blast of water, or use dormant oil in early spring or light horticultural oil in summer.

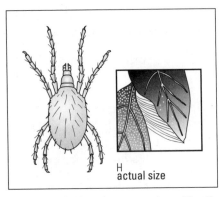

actual size

Figure 8-5: Spider mites are easier to identify by the damage they do than by sight.

Tarnished plant bugs (lygus bugs)

These ¼-inch-long (0.6 cm), yellow-to-brown plant eaters attack many kinds of plants — more than 400, including some of our most important economic crops — leaving behind dark, sunken leaf spots and wilting or dead shoots. They especially like the growing points of apples and strawberries. Catch them with white sticky traps. Prevent problems by covering susceptible plants with a floating row cover.

Tent caterpillars

These caterpillars form tentlike webs full of teeming caterpillars on trees and shrubs. In large numbers, they can defoliate an entire tree. Knock caterpillars off severely infested branches with a broom or pole.

Tomato hornworms

This large, 3- to 5-inch-long (7.5–12.5 cm), green caterpillar is notable particularly for its white stripes and the threatening "horn" protruding from its rear. As dangerous as it appears, the horn can do no harm, which is why handpicking is one of the preferred controls. If you have lots of tomatoes (or peppers or potatoes), you may want to spray or dust with Bt in late spring or early summer. Bt is effective as long as worms remain small. Several tiny wasps also parasitize this caterpillar.

Whiteflies

Whiteflies look like small, white gnats, but they suck plant sap and can proliferate in warm climates or greenhouses. They can also spread diseases with their sucking mouthparts. Trap whiteflies with yellow sticky traps. Cure infestations with regular sprays of hot (150°F/66°C) water (directly from your water heater to your infested plants), insecticidal soap, light horticultural oil, or pyrethrin. Be sure to treat leaf undersides where whiteflies and their larvae reside.

Managing Pests

Think of pest management as a staircase. On the first step you can find the least disruptive, innocuous actions, and on the top step are the most toxic and the most potentially harmful measures. The best way to control pests is to start at the bottom and move up the stairs only when absolutely necessary. This strategy is called *integrated pest management* (IPM). This approach takes advantage of the complex interrelationships between insects and plants to find the least toxic ways to reduce damage to crops.

The following list outlines the actions you can take in your garden to keep a pest from getting the upper hand. The measures move from the least aggressive and potentially harmful to the most aggressive.

- ✔ **Strong blast from a hose** that knocks small pests such as aphids and spider mites off your plants. Spraying daily can provide good control.

- ✔ **Barriers** such as *floating row covers* (translucent, lightweight fabrics that cover plants) that keep flying insects from reaching plants; cutworm collars placed around seedlings; and copper strips that encircle plants and give slugs an electric shock. Make cutworm collars with 4-inch-high (10 cm) rings pushed 2 inches (5 cm) into the soil; use toilet tissue rolls or rolled newspaper.

✔ **Insect traps** that use chemical attractants and colors to lure pests, such as sticky, red balls for apple maggots.

✔ **Bacterial insecticides,** such as *Bacillus thuringiensis* (Bt) for caterpillars, and milky spore disease for soil-dwelling grubs.

✔ **Least toxic controls,** such as insecticidal soaps, horticultural oils, and rotenone insecticides, which kill pests but cause minimal impact on the environment.

✔ **Botanical insecticides,** such as neem.

Encouraging "good" insects

The average square yard of garden contains more than a thousand insects. Some are plant pollinators, some help break down organic matter, and some prey on other more damaging ones. Only a small proportion of the insects cause much damage to your plants.

Beneficial insects prey upon or parasitize garden pests. In nature, beneficial insects keep plant-eating pests under control.

Here are some beneficial bugs and insects that you'll want to keep around your yard:

✔ **Lady beetles:** You're probably aware of the ladybug's voracious appetite for aphids. Both larva and adult stages prey on pests. One ladybug can dine on 40 to 50 aphids a day. Ladybugs also prey on mites and other soft-bodied insects.

✔ **Green lacewing:** Larval-stage lacewings feed on aphids, thrips, mites, and various other insect eggs; overall, the most useful insect in home gardens. Both larva and adult stages are beneficial, but the larva much more so.

✔ **Trichogramma wasps:** These tiny wasps parasitize many kinds of caterpillars by laying eggs in them. The wasps are effective against corn earworm, loopers, and tomato hornworm. They cannot attack people in any way.

✔ **Parasitic nematodes:** The tiny worms parasitize many soil-dwelling and burrowing insects, such as grubs, cutworms, and weevils. These are different from the pest nematodes that feed on plant roots.

> ✔ **Chinese praying mantis.** This general predator is inter-
> esting to watch but doesn't provide reliable control of
> pests.

All these beneficial insects are available from mail-order gardening companies. Each has special requirements in terms of
the best time to release them into the garden. Whether you
choose to buy beneficials or rely on the ones already present
in your yard, you can take steps to encourage them to stick
around:

> ✔ **Avoid indiscriminate pesticide spraying, which kills
> beneficials as well as pests.** If you must spray, choose a
> product that specifically targets the pests you want to
> eliminate, and use it when it will be least harmful. For
> example, sprays that are harmful to bees can be used in
> the evening after bees have returned to the hive.
>
> ✔ **Make sure that the beneficials have plenty to eat by
> allowing small numbers of pests to reside in your
> garden.** If you release ladybugs before you've even spot-
> ted aphids, they may move elsewhere to find food.
>
> ✔ **Provide beneficials with shelter.** Grow a variety of
> plants — tall, short, spreading, and upright — to give the
> insects many potential homes.
>
> ✔ **Many beneficials also feed on nectar and pollen, so
> grow flowers such as Queen Anne's lace and evening
> primrose.** Lacewings love fennel, caraway, and dill.
> Goldenrod has been found to attract more than 75 differ-
> ent species of beneficial insects.

Safe and effective pest chemicals

Gardeners today have at their disposal a handful of effective
and safe pesticides. All the following are approved for use by
certified organic farmers.

Bacillus thuringiensis (Bt)

Bt exists naturally in most soils. Different strains of Bt occur
that produce protein crystals that are toxic to certain insects.
The strain for most caterpillars is *B. t. kurstaki.* Commercially
prepared Bt spray or powder has no effect on adult butterflies
or moths. Remember, however, that not all caterpillars are

pests. Strains of Bt have been developed for a few other pests. Some leaf-feeding beetles (including Colorado potato beetles) are susceptible to *B. t. tenebrionis,* for example.

Advantages: One advantage is safety — Bt is essentially non-toxic to humans, other mammals, and birds. The label specifies no waiting period between application and harvest. Bt is also highly selective and easily incorporated with existing natural controls.

Disadvantages: A limitation of Bt is its slow action. After pests consume it, their feeding slows down. But their deaths may not occur for two to five days. Bt also breaks down quickly — if the caterpillars don't eat some while it's fresh, it probably won't work.

Because Bt is a near-perfect insecticide, there is danger of overuse. Any overused insecticide gradually becomes less effective as insects evolve defenses to it. Some insect pests, such as the diamondback moth and Indian meal moth, were once susceptible and are now at least partially immune to Bt.

How to use: Use Bt against cabbageworms, cutworms, and other caterpillars. Use *B. t. tenebrionis* against Colorado potato beetles. The bacterial toxin causes caterpillar death two to five days after it is eaten; the toxin dissipates in two days or less. It is available as liquid spray or dust. Apply in late afternoon and reapply after rain. Repeat applications as needed. Mix with insecticidal soap for greater effectiveness.

Diatomaceous earth (DE)

Diatomaceous earth, or DE, is a powderlike dust made of the silicate skeletons of tiny water creatures called *diatoms.* Millions of years ago, as the diatoms died, their skeletons gradually accumulated into deep layers that are mined today from deposits where oceans or large lakes once covered the land. DE acts like ground glass, cutting into the waxy coat of many kinds of insects and causing them to dry out and die. DE is often combined with the botanical insecticide, pyrethrin (described in this section). The addition of pyrethrin makes DE more lethal for many insects.

Advantages: Easy to handle and apply. DE is not toxic and leaves no residue.

Disadvantages: DE is not selective and kills spiders and beneficial insects as well as pests. DE is available in two forms. One, which is used primarily in swimming pool filters, is not an effective insecticide and is dangerous to inhale (it can cause a lung disease called silicosis). In your garden, use only the natural grade of DE. Always wear goggles and a dust mask during application.

How to use: Dust DE onto leaves and stems to control pests such as aphids, immature Colorado potato beetles, immature forms of squash bug, immature Mexican bean beetles, and whiteflies. Sometimes a band of DE makes an effective slug and snail barrier. It works best in dry situations; reapply after rain.

One of the most convenient applicators of small amounts of DE is the Spritzer tube duster. This applicator holds a small amount of dust and dispenses it with a pump action. It's available from Perma-Guard Inc., 2430 Alamo SE, Suite 102, Albuquerque, NM 87106 (phone: 505-243-1460; Web: www.perma-guard.com). The Cadillac of dust applicators is the Dustin-Mizer. It holds a pound of dust in a canister and dispenses with a hand crank.

Horticultural oils

Horticultural oils are most often highly refined extracts of crude oil. (Some vegetable oils, such as cottonseed and soybean oil, are also sometimes used.) They kill insects by plugging the pores through which the insects breathe.

Advantages: These oils are increasingly recommended for vegetable garden pest control because they present few risks to either gardeners or desirable species and integrate well with natural biological controls. Also, oils dissipate quickly through evaporation, leaving little residue.

Disadvantages: Oils can damage plants if applied at excessive rates or on particularly hot (above 100°F/38°C) or cold (below 40°F/5°C) days.

How to use: Spray oils in vegetable gardens to kill aphids, leafhoppers, spider mites, and whiteflies. A few drops of oil in the ear tips of corn control corn earworm.

Use highly refined horticultural oils and dilute according to label directions. Do not apply oils to drought-stressed plants, or on hot, cold, or very humid days. Don't apply horticultural oils to green plants at rates recommended for leafless, dormant plants.

Insecticidal soaps

Insecticidal soaps are specific fatty acids that have been found by experiment to be toxic to pests, primarily soft-bodied insects like aphids, mealybugs, spider mites, and whiteflies. Surprisingly, adult Japanese beetles are also susceptible.

Advantages: Insecticidal soap is one of the safest insecticides. Most nontarget insects are unaffected, and the soaps are not toxic to animals. Soap insecticides act fast and leave no residue. You can use them on vegetables up to the moment of harvest.

Disadvantages: Soaps readily burn some plants such as peas, and the effectiveness of the soap diminishes greatly when mixed with hard water (water high in dissolved minerals). Soaps kill pests only when they make direct contact.

How to use: Use against aphids, earwigs, grasshoppers, Japanese beetles (adults), leafhoppers, spider mites, and whiteflies. Apply diluted concentrate or ready-to-use liquid when the air is still. To improve effectiveness, mix with warm, soft water and be sure to cover both sides of leaves. Reapply after rain. Can burn leaves of certain plants during hot weather.

Neem

Neem is an extract derived from the crushed seeds of the tropical neem tree *(Azadirachta indica)*. Though intensely studied for many years now, it is still a new botanical insecticide. The primary active ingredient is the compound azadirachtin. Two forms are commonly available. One is a 3 percent solution of azadirachtin, the most insecticidal component, and the other is "clarified hydrophobic extracts of neem seeds," essentially a syrupy oil (make sure the oil is warm before mixing with water).

Both forms of neem work as both an insecticide and an agent that prevents insects from feeding. They also kill insects in the juvenile stage by thwarting their development and are most effective against aphids, thrips, and whiteflies. Neem oil is also fungicidal and can control black spot of roses, powdery mildew, and rust diseases.

Advantages: Neem has no measurable toxicity to mammals. (In some countries, neem extract is considered healthful to people and is added to various food and personal products.) The Environmental Protection Agency (EPA) stipulated that neem was exempt from food crop tolerances because it is considered nontoxic.

Disadvantages: Neem doesn't have a quick "knock-down" effect, but a week or so after application, you'll notice a steady decline in the number of pests. It is not effective against adult insects (though it may interfere with egg production) and has little impact on beneficial insects. Once beetle numbers build up on the plant, neem no longer discourages them.

How to use: Neem sprays degrade very quickly in water. Mix only the amount you need and apply all of it immediately. Reapply after rainfall. On the plant, neem retains its activity against juvenile insect pests for about one week. Use neem to kill juvenile aphids, Colorado potato beetles, and thrips, and to repel whiteflies, Japanese beetles, and adult Colorado potato beetles. Apply liquid spray morning or evening when humidity is highest. Repeat weekly; spray lasts on plants about one week. As a toxin, apply when pests are young. As an antifeedant, neem is effective against Japanese beetles; apply before the pests appear.

To mix neem oil with water, the oil needs to be at least room temperature. But neem mixes still better if you warm it first in water on the stove, or even in the microwave for about 30 seconds. If you try the latter, be sure to remove the aluminum seal under the cap first.

Pyrethrins

Derived from the painted daisy, *Tanacetum cinerariifolium*, pyrethrins are considered one of the most important natural insecticides. When you must either use a broad-spectrum insecticide in the vegetable garden or lose the crop, pyrethrins are among your best choices.

Broad-spectrum insecticides are products that kill a diversity of insects — pest and beneficial alike. If you need to use an insecticide to control a particular pest, use a product that targets that particular kind of pest without harming beneficial insects. The terminology can be confusing, however. Pyrethrum is the ground-up flowers of the daisy. *Pyrethrins* (most always plural) are the insecticidal components of the flowers. *Pyrethroids,* such as cypermethrin, permethrin, and resmethrin, are synthetic compounds that resemble pyrethrins but are more toxic and persistent.

Advantages: Pyrethrins are of low toxicity to mammals and kill insects quickly. In sunlight, they break down and are non-toxic within a day or less.

Disadvantages: Often, pure pyrethrins only stun insects, which is why they often get combined with a *synergist* (a chemical that enhances the effectiveness of the active ingredients) such as piperonyl butoxide or with another botanical insecticide, such as rotenone. Also, pyrethrin is toxic to honeybees — apply it in the evening after bees are in their hives.

How to use: Use against most vegetable garden pests, such as flea, potato, and bean beetles, including the hard-to-kill pests, such as beetles, squash bugs, and tarnished plant bugs. For best results, apply in the late afternoon or evening. Pyrethrins degrade within one day.

Rotenone

Rotenone is often recommended for organic gardeners because of its botanical origin (derived from the roots of tropical legumes).

Advantages: It is approved for use in organic gardens and breaks down quickly in sunlight.

Disadvantages: Rotenone is toxic to pests and beneficials alike.

How to use: Use this broad-spectrum insecticide as a last resort against cabbageworms, Colorado potato beetles, flea beetles, fruit worms, Japanese beetles, loopers, Mexican bean beetles, thrips, and weevils. Apply in early evening when bees are inactive. It remains toxic up to one week.

Several other types of pesticides are available at nurseries and home centers, but we regard some of them with suspicion and a few with scorn. Our advice: If a pest problem is so resistant to any of these materials and so bothersome, call a professional. Check with your cooperative extension agent first. Consider hiring a professional pest control applicator to spray.

Preventing Plant Diseases

Many plant diseases are difficult — in some cases impossible — to cure. If you suspect that a certain disease is going to show up on your prized plant, such as black spot on roses, you can take steps to prevent infection. Find out when that disease is most likely to strike. Then identify the best product to use and apply it according to recommendations on the label.

When you spot a disease on your plants, try to identify it with the help of reference books or personnel at a local nursery, garden center, botanical garden, or extension service office. Occasionally, you can get products to eradicate or prevent further spread of the disease. At the very least, adapt the following cultural techniques to make your garden less susceptible to disease damage.

Solarization

You can cook the disease right out of your soil by a process called *solarization.* To do this, first cultivate the soil and get it ready for planting. Then moisten the soil to a depth of 2 feet (61 cm). Cover the area with a sheet of 2- to 4-mils-thick, clear, UV-stabilized plastic and secure the edges so that air can't leak. The heat of the sun will raise the temperature underneath high enough to kill many disease organisms (and weeds) that are contained in the upper several inches of soil. Leave the plastic on for one or two months, and then remove it and plant. Don't cultivate again before planting, or you run the risk of bringing pathogens up to the surface again.

Solarization is most effective if done during the hottest part of the year. Southern gardeners will reap the most benefit from this process, but northerners can increase the heat by using double layers of plastic or by spreading chicken manure or another hot manure on the soil before laying down the plastic.

More than a dozen dirty diseases: What to do

In the following sections, we provide some tips on how to prevent, identify, and — if possible — treat some common plant diseases.

Anthracnose

This fungus can attack many trees, including dogwoods and sycamores, as well as tomatoes and melons. It begins by producing small, discolored leaf spots or dead twigs, which can spread to become serious. Avoid by choosing resistant plants. Destroy fallen diseased leaves and dead branches and twigs. Hire an arborist to spray trees that have had the disease three consecutive years. Consider removing susceptible trees and replanting with resistant varieties.

Apple scab

This fungus attacks apple and crab apple trees, producing discolored leaf spots and woody-brown fruit lesions. Avoid by planting scab-resistant varieties. Rake up and destroy leaves in fall to reduce the number of overwintering spores. Susceptible varieties need a preventive spray program during wet spring weather to prevent reinfection.

Spray sulfur, copper, or *Bordeaux mixture* (a mixture of copper sulfate, lime, and water) as a protective spray at the beginning of scab season (once flower buds in spring), then two or three more times at approximately weekly intervals.

Black spot

This rose disease causes black spots on foliage and can spread, causing complete defoliation. Avoid problems by growing disease-resistant roses and cleaning up and destroying any diseased leaves that fall to the ground. To prevent black spot on susceptible roses, use a preventive fungicide spray during damp weather. Sprays of captan, copper, or lime-sulfur are most effective. Also try potassium bicarbonate (or baking soda — sodium bicarbonate) at the rate of 1 table-spoon each per gallon of water, weekly or after rain. Apply in morning and not during periods of hottest weather. Neem oil is also effective.

Botrytis blight

This fungus attacks a wide variety of plants, including peonies, tulips, geraniums, and strawberries. It causes discolored patches on foliage, browning and droopy stalks on flowers, and premature rotting of fruits. Discourage botrytis by allowing air to circulate freely around susceptible plants. Remove and destroy any infected plant parts. Spray emerging peony shoots in early spring with copper sulfate.

Brown rot

This fungus disease is common on peaches, nectarines, and other stone fruits. Brown rot can attack flowers and fruit, ultimately coating the infected parts with brown spores. The fruit rots and shrivels. To avoid, select disease-resistant plants or at least less-susceptible types. Remove and destroy infected plant parts. You'll probably also need a preventive spray program.

Cytospora canker

This bacterial disease attacks woody stems on susceptible plants, such as fruit trees, spruces, and maples, forming cankers that can kill infected branches. To avoid, plant resistant or less-susceptible plants. If possible, remove and destroy infected branches.

Damping-off

This fungus disease attacks the base of seedling stems, cutting the stem off from the roots. Avoid damping-off by sowing seeds in sterile seed-sowing mix and spacing the seeds so that they don't come up in a crowded mass. Cover the seeds thinly with finely shredded sphagnum moss, which has natural antibiotic action that helps prevent disease. Keep the soil moist but not soggy.

Mildew (downy and powdery)

These two fungi produce similar symptoms: white, powdery coating on leaves. A variety of plants are susceptible, including roses, grapes, bee balms, zinnias, and lilacs, but a different kind of mildew attacks each kind of plant. A mildew that attacks lilacs won't harm roses. The fungi disfigure plants but may not kill them outright. Instead, they weaken plants, making them unattractive and susceptible to other problems. Downy mildew attacks during cool, wet weather; powdery mildew (shown in Figure 8-6) comes later in the season during warm, humid weather and cool nights. Avoid downy mildew by planting resistant plants and by not getting the leaves wet. Use drip irrigation. Avoid powdery mildew by planting resistant plants.

Figure 8-6: Powdery mildew thrives during warm, humid days and cool nights.

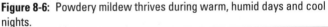

Peach leaf curl

This fungal disease overwinters on peach tree-twigs and migrates to the emerging leaves in humid, wet weather when temperatures are between 50°F and 60°F (10°C and 16°C). The leaves curl, turn red, and eventually die. Typically, the disease develops early the first year, and the tree may grow through it and appear fine. But when the disease becomes established, the leaf curl returns and gets progressively worse each year. Eventually, the tree becomes debilitated. When you see the symptoms, it's too late to stop the organism that season.

You can control peach leaf curl with one or, at most, two applications. First, spray a fungicide such as lime-sulfur or Bordeaux mix in fall when the trees are *dormant* (leafless). For extra insurance, spray again in early spring before leaves emerge.

Phytophthora blight

This bacterial disease attacks a variety of plants, including rhododendrons. It causes leaves to discolor and stems to die, often killing the entire plant. Another form can cause root rot and rapid plant death. Start with healthy plants and provide them with well-drained soil. Work bark into the soil; it seems to discourage the fungus. Try not to wet the foliage in the afternoon or evening.

Rust

This fungus disease is easy to identify: It forms a rusty coating on the foliage of susceptible plants, like roses, snapdragons, hollyhocks, and blackberry (see Figure 8-7). Avoid susceptible plants or look for disease-resistant varieties. Provide good air circulation. Remove and destroy infected parts.

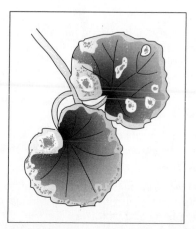

Figure 8-7: Rust is an easily identified fungus.

Sooty mold

Insect pests that release sticky drops of honeydew, such as aphids, encourage this harmless but unattractive fungus disease. The black-colored mold grows on the honeydew, a sure sign that sucking insects are at work. Rinse off the mold and sap with soapy water and then control the insect pests.

Wilt (fusarium and verticillium)

These soil-borne fungus diseases cause susceptible plants such as tomatoes, peppers, melons, cabbages, and strawberries to suffer leaf yellowing, wilting, and often death. The fungus survives many years in the soil without a host. Grow wilt-resistant or wilt-tolerant varieties. Resistant tomato varieties have the letters *VF* as part of their name.

Least-toxic disease remedies

Use the following fungicides to make a protective coating on susceptible plants. Most are certified by organic gardening groups and are widely available at nurseries and garden centers.

- **Sulfur:** This naturally occurring mineral is nontoxic but is a potential skin and eye irritant. You can buy sulfur in powder or liquid form. Powders can be applied with a dust applicator, or mixed with water according to label directions.

- **Lime sulfur:** Powerful and caustic but highly effective for some problems, lime sulfur can burn the leaves of some plants.

- **Copper:** This strong, broad-spectrum spray can be toxic to some plants, especially when overused. Use only as a last resort.

- **Bordeaux mixture:** A mix of copper and sulfur, this old-time fungicide is less toxic than pure copper but has the same limitations.

- **Remedy fungicide:** Harmless as baking soda, the key ingredient, this spray controls a range of fungal diseases on ornamental plants and fruit trees.

Outwitting animals

If you've ever had a newly planted garden decimated by a groundhog, then you know just how long it takes to drive to the store, buy fencing, rush home, and install it. Whether it be greedy groundhogs, nibbling rabbits, browsing deer, or gophers and moles tunneling throughout your yard, animals can be a nemesis to gardeners.

The irony is that the nearby woods or fields or open space that attracted you to living in your home in the first place also provides habitat for many of the animals that plague you. You may, in fact, have moved into their territory.

When trying to coexist with wild animals, the first priority is to keep your sense of humor. Beyond that, you can use a few techniques to protect some of that garden produce for you to enjoy. If you don't succeed with one method, try another. The following suggestions are grouped according to the type of animal:

✔ **Deer:** Deer are creatures of habit. They often travel along the same routes day after day, moving between two locations. Build a deer-excluding fence about 8 feet (2.5 m) high (deer have been known to jump 10-foot/3 m fences). Before you invest in a fence, you may want to try surrounding your garden with a heavy fishing line attached to posts at about 3 feet (1 m) high. This can startle deer because they don't see the fishing line, and they may retreat. This isn't a method to try with young children around — they could injure themselves on the line.

Deer avoid some plants, although they are notorious for changing their minds about what they want for dinner. In general, pungent or fuzzy-leafed plants are safe.

✔ **Gophers:** These are burrowing, antisocial rodents that can carve out 700 square yards (585 m^2)of elaborate underground tunnels. While they tunnel, they work up quite an appetite, and any plant roots that happen to be in the way turn into lunch.

Underground barriers made of hardware cloth are effective. Install barriers at least 2 feet (60 cm) deep to block their borrowing.

Various traps are available to catch gophers dead or alive, and traps are the only method used by orchardists and others who are serious about limiting gopher damage. Traps work best when set inside the tunnels.

(continued)

(continued)

- **Groundhogs (woodchucks):** The easiest way to eliminate groundhogs is a fence, one that extends 3 to 4 feet (1–1.2 m) above ground and 18 inches (46 cm) below ground. Traps are next best. Groundhogs are among the easier garden raiders to trap alive with a Havahart trap. Check with local and state ordinances about any restrictions on live trapping, and take care when releasing any wild animal so that it doesn't turn on you.

If you're at your wit's end dealing with marauding deer, gophers, or woodchucks, consult your local animal control officer. Normally, you'll find these folks listed under the city, county, or state listings in the telephone book. Another resource is the book *Outwitting Critters: A Humane Guide for Confronting Devious Animals and Winning,* by Bill Adler, Jr.

Chapter 9

Winning the War against Weeds

In This Chapter

▶ Knowing what kind of weeds you're dealing with

▶ Keeping weeds from muscling out your plants

*T*he challenge of combating pests and diseases (see Chapter 8) is fraught with unknowns: What works today might not work tomorrow. As soon as you let down your guard, your plants get chewed to nubs. Weeds, however, have an element that is much more predictable and comforting: Weeds don't change their minds. You can always count on weeds to behave in a certain way, and there is one strategy that always works: pulling.

Of course, we're not talking here about fields full of wild brambles that you're trying to eliminate. We're talking about common weeds that you are likely to find in your lawn and garden. You can use some general techniques that can make your yard less attractive to weeds. In this chapter, we show you how.

Weed-Control Basics

The principle is pretty simple: Stop the weeds before they start. Okay, prevention isn't so simple in many situations. But if you can take sometimes very minor steps before the weeds take hold, you can avoid the really big jobs when they do.

✔ **Use mulch.** No matter what kind of mulch you use, it cuts down on weed growth. A thick mulch for garden pathways and between beds can be made quite easily from layers of newspapers topped with straw or hay. At season's end, you can till the mulch into the garden to provide organic matter.

✔ **Prior to planting, *cultivate* (loosen the soil) to expose weed seeds to sunlight and start them growing.** After a couple of weeks, you can pull the weeds or till them under and thus eliminate some major competition for your plants.

✔ **Cover your crops.** Being patient when preparing a garden bed can pay off big time later on. You can dramatically reduce weeds in your newly dug garden by sowing a cover crop such as buckwheat the summer before you plant the garden. The buckwheat grows so densely that it outcompetes the weeds. When you till the buckwheat under, it also enriches the soil with organic matter. Then you can plant another cover crop such as annual rye in the fall, which you can till under the following spring. Your garden will then be practically weed-free and ready to plant. Alternatively, you can plant a late garden after you till under the buckwheat.

✔ **Place landscape fabrics on the soil after planting trees and shrubs, and then top with mulch.** Annual weeds are successfully impeded, woody perennials less so. Fabric brands include Typar, Weed Block, Weed-X, and Mulch Plus.

✔ **Hand-hoe and pull weeds.** Not glamorous but still one of the most effective means for most small home gardens, the key is to yank the weeds while they're young.

✔ **Solarize.** Follow the directions given in Chapter 8.

The most critical time to control weeds is during the first few weeks after transplanting or sowing seed. As long as you help your plants get off to a good start, they'll have a fighting chance of producing a crop of food or flowers in spite of future competing weeds.

Nontoxic Herbicides

With several effective alternatives to toxic pesticides on the market, you can avoid their risks and, in some cases, even fertilize your garden at the same time. Here are some choices:

- **Corn gluten weed killer** is available under several brand names, such as A-maizing Lawn, WOW (With-out-weeds), and WeedzSTOP. This product is a highly concentrated protein extract of cornmeal. Applied in early spring and again in early August, it will prevent seed growth for up to six weeks. Because it will also kill other seeds, avoid using it in vegetable gardens and on new lawns. As an added bonus, the cornmeal provides nitrogen fertilizer.

- **Weed Eraser** is made from pelargonic acid, a fatty acid found in crops such as apples, carrots, and grapes. It lowers the pH enough to kill broadleaf weeds, such as pigweed and dandelions, in two hours.

Common Weeds

If you remember nothing else about controlling weeds, keep this strategy in mind at all times: Remove perennial weeds as soon as you spot them, and pull annual weeds before they flower. Treat biennials as perennials.

Bindweed (Convolvulus arvensis)

Spreading from underground roots, this vining perennial can snake around your garden and wrap itself around your plants. The leaves are shaped like an arrowhead and the flowers resemble morning glories, a more appreciated cousin. Beware, however, that if you allow bindweed to flower, you greatly compound your problem. The seeds have been found to be viable after 50 years. To remove the plants, use a digging fork rather than a spade, which can divide the roots into pieces that will each grow new plants.

Repeated *flaming* is an effective control strategy for bindweed. Cook your weeds to death. With a propane torch in hand, you can kill weeds in $\frac{1}{10}$ of a second by boiling the water in the plant's cells until they burst. Flaming is most effective in spring and early summer against annual weeds. Perennial weeds may require several treatments. Follow all safety precautions, of course, if you use this method.

Bermuda grass (Cynodon dactylon)

This wiry perennial grass (see Figure 9-1) has thin blades with creases down the center. Its creeping stems travel quickly, rooting at the nodes. Any piece of stem or root left behind after you weed can establish a new plant. Bermuda grass has a secret weapon to reduce competition from nearby plants: It releases a chemical to impede their growth. Flaming provides good control.

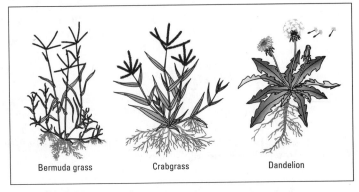

Bermuda grass   Crabgrass   Dandelion

Figure 9-1: Common weeds.

Chickweed (Stellaria media)

You can easily spot this densely matting annual weed in late winter and early spring, when the stems of ½-inch (1.2 cm) oval leaves reach toward the sun. The tiny white flowers open fully on sunny days. Broken stems can root if dropped on the ground.

Crabgrass (Digitaria)

Most common in dry, sandy soil, this annual has leaves with a bluish cast and spreading stems that root at the nodes.

(Refer to Figure 9-1.) It's easy to grab hold of the clump and pull it up. Mulch effectively smothers crabgrass. Control by maintaining a vigorous lawn and by applying corn gluten meal in early spring.

Curly dock (Rumex crispus)

Perennial curly dock often arrives in gardens courtesy of manure. Left alone, it grows to 4 feet (1.2 m) tall with clusters of heart-shaped, reddish-brown seed pods. The taproot can extend 2 feet (60 cm) underground, but if you can remove just the top 5 inches (12.5 cm), the root dies. Corn gluten herbicide prevents seeds from sprouting.

Dandelion (Taraxacum officinale)

The first leaves of this perennial, which emerge in early spring, are low and oval. Later leaves are arrow-shaped with deep lopes. The unmistakable yellow flowers quickly go to seed, so pick them early. The edible flowers are reported to be tasty when battered and fried. Long-handled weeders seem made to remove this common weed from lawns and gardens. Remove as much of the taproot as possible because the plant regrows from any portion that's left. Corn gluten herbicide prevents seed germination, and Weed Eraser can kill adult weeds.

Lamb's-quarters (Chenopodium album)

This upright-growing annual is distinctive for the white sparkles on the surfaces of young leaves. Leaf undersides are dusty white. Adding to the rather attractive display, the stems are often red or lighter green. Frequent hand-pulling and hoeing can keep the rapidly growing weed under control. Prevent seed germination with corn gluten herbicide.

Oxalis

This is a perennial weed notable for its clover-like leaves and bright yellow flowers. Control by repeated cultivations or flaming and applications of corn gluten herbicide. Use the corn gluten later to minimize or prevent seed germination.

Purslane (Portulaca oleracea)

Think of the popular bedding plant called portulaca and you'll be able to identify annual purslane. The succulent leaves are prostrate and branching, forming dense mats. Pulling and cultivation help, but plants reroot readily. Or use Safer's SuperFast soap herbicide to spray. Corn gluten herbicide prevents seed growth.

Redroot pigweed (Amaranthus retroflexus)

The reddish stems of this annual can grow up to 10 feet (3 m) tall, with oblong, pointy leaves. Green, upright flowers resemble a bottle brush. These plants are quite easy to pull, but they also reroot easily, so uprooting them and then leaving them in the garden won't help much. As for all annuals, slice them off at the surface with a sharp scuffle hoe. Or use Safer's SuperFast herbicide or Weed Eraser to kill pigweed. Corn gluten herbicide prevents its seeds from germinating.

Shepherd's purse (Capsella bursa-pastoris)

Seed pods of this annual are thought to resemble the purses carried by early shepherds. These tiny green triangles perch on thin stalks all along upright stems that emerge from the base of the plant, which resembles a dandelion. Remove seed pods before they drop seeds or you'll never get rid of these weeds.

Spotted (or prostrate) spurge

This very low growing and spreading annual weed loves hot weather and compacted soil. Eliminate by cultivating, flaming, or using soap herbicide. Prevent seed germination with corn gluten herbicide.

Chapter 10

Ten (Or So) Tips for Gardening in Tight Spaces

In This Chapter

▶ Designing in limited space

▶ Making small seem big

▶ Discovering hidden growing spots

*J*ust because your outdoor space is small doesn't mean you have to give up your dreams of having a truly satisfying garden. In fact, if you've ever lingered in a small garden that is well-planned and carefully put together, you've probably noticed that the garden has a sense of intimacy and enclosure that most large, sprawling landscapes lack.

Smallness need not dictate the type of gardening that you do. Whether you're aiming for a serene Japanese-style meditation garden or the country charm of an English cottage garden, the basic techniques for successful small-space gardening are the same. The following tips can help you on your way.

Keep It Simple

A small garden feels most spacious and harmonious when the design is simple and all the elements work together. Choose a single style or theme for your garden and use this style to connect all the parts, from paving to plants and structures and ornaments. Just imagine how distracting a spewing Goliath of a fountain would be in a tiny, contemplative Japanese-style garden. In contrast, a bamboo spout trickling water onto stone would feel soothing and appear quite natural in such a setting.

To help keep things simple and avoid a hodgepodge, repeat garden elements. For example, instead of planting a wide assortment, use a few types of plants repeatedly in different areas of the garden. Rely on two or three colors that best express the garden's mood. Choose one or two types of paving for walkways and use those same materials throughout the garden to create a visual, as well as physical, connection.

Pay Attention to the Details

In a little garden, everything shows. Each plant, ornament, structure, and surface becomes an integral part of the whole. One goal of small-garden design is to create interest and intrigue without adding extraneous *stuff*.

One of the advantages of smallness is that it encourages you to focus on quality rather than quantity. Just a few carefully chosen and well-placed plants or ornaments can transform an otherwise bland plot into an evocative haven. Consider using the following lures (and invent some of your own) to attract attention and to keep the viewer from taking in your entire garden in one glance:

- A bent-willow chair flanked by a large pot of tulips in bloom

- A wall-mounted fountain (saves more space than a free-standing one)

- An ornamental waterspout protruding from a wall and flowing onto a pebble surface

- A small pond in a large antique ceramic pot

- A stone sculpture

- A clipped boxwood topiary

- ✔ A single raised urn set in brick paving and filled with white, daisylike marguerites and geraniums at the urn's base

- ✔ An apple tree trained to a decorative pattern against a fence or wall

Vary Levels

Add vertical texture to the garden by using berms, steps, or terraces. Changes in levels add dimension and lengthen the route through the garden, which makes the space appear bigger. Level changes also divert the eye from the garden's boundaries and add an element of surprise as you move through the garden.

Try Some Visual Trickery

Visual trickery lies at the very heart of successful small-space gardening. Employ the following strategies to help defy garden boundaries and make your small space feel larger:

- ✔ **Use plants to blur walls and fences.** Doing so ensures that your eye doesn't abruptly stop at the garden's boundaries.

- ✔ **Construct gently curving paths.** By curving your paths, you can make them "disappear" at the garden's edge (perhaps at a false gate in a fence) to suggest that more lies beyond.

- ✔ **Create depth.** Layer plants at the garden's periphery. Put light-colored or variegated plants in front of taller, darker green ones. Or place shrubs or small trees in front of a vine-covered wall or fence.

- ✔ **Position cool colors.** Use cool colors, such as blue and violet, toward the farthest edges of the garden. These colors tend to recede and give an impression of distance.

- ✔ **Install a wall-mounted mirror.** Such a mirror can reflect an intriguing view.

- ✔ **Draw attention inward and downward.** Use decorative paving or an eye-catching living ground cover.

Borrow a View

Expand the boundaries of your garden visually to incorporate a view beyond your property line into your garden design. If, for example, your neighbor has a gorgeous flowering shade tree, situate a bench in your yard to take advantage of the view.

Plant in Gaps

Gardening in the crevices between bricks or stone not only gives you more growing space but also softens the hard look of these surfaces. Plants growing between paving create a visual link, connecting the hard surfaces with adjacent flower beds or other plantings.

Good gap-plant choices provide a thick, low carpet of greenery that stands up to some foot traffic. Certain ground covers add flowers or fragrance, as well.

Cover Up with Climbers

Save valuable ground space by growing plants vertically. Use annual or perennial climbers or use *wall shrubs* — shrubs you can prune until they are nearly flat against a wall.

Plant Overhead

Encourage plants up and over arbors and arches to create a cool, green ceiling or a dramatic canopy of blooms. Deciduous plants provide welcome filtered shade in summer and let the warming sun shine through in winter.

Start with simple, sturdy structures that can support the weight and bulk of heavy, woody vines at maturity. A classic plant for garden ceilings is wisteria with its fragrant violet flowers in 1½-foot-long (46 cm) clusters. Among edibles, the kiwi vine (with branches to 30 feet/9 m long) is a favorite patio cover. Keep in mind that both of these vines are rampant growers, so they require sturdy supports.

Use lightweight containers to suspend plants from tree branches or overhead structures.

Be Choosey about What You Include in Your Garden

Select plants for your small garden as though you were choosing gems for your lover. A plant with the right style, fit, size, and color has the potential to dazzle, just as an inappropriate choice will look and feel awkward. When you select plants, consider the big picture — consider how each plant will contribute to the whole.

Even with room for only a few containers and a chair, your garden can be inspiring and satisfying. So go forth and seek out the nooks and crannies.

Index

• A •

acidity
  pH balance adjustments, 56–57
  soil pH factors, 51–52
action hoes, purchasing, 30
activators, compost starter, 121
aerating tool, compost piles, 121
AHS (American Horticultural
    Society), 16–18
'Alderman,' pea variety, 88
alkalinity
  pH balance adjustments, 56–57
  soil pH factors, 51–52
alpine, winter injury prevention, 25
Amaranthus retroflexus (redroot
    pigweed), herbicides, 158
amendments, soil, 52–58, 84–85
American Horticultural Society
    (AHS), Heat-Zone Map, 16–18
anaerobic containers, compost,
    120
Animal and Plant Health Inspection
    Service (APHIS), 132
annuals, spacing guidelines, 65
anthracnose, 146
anvil pruners, 30
aphids, 126
apple maggots, 126–127
apple scab, 146
apples, 92–96
arborvitae, winter injury, 26
automated watering systems, 106
Azadirachta indica (neem tree),
    142–143
azalea, 26, 77

• B •

Bacillus thuringiensis (Bt), 138–140
bacterial insecticides, 138
balled-and-burlapped plants, 64,
    75–77
barberry, multiseason shrub, 77
bare-root plants, 64, 74–75
bark, girding prevention, 26–27
barriers
  insect controls, 131
  pest management method, 137
  polyester bird netting, 98
basil, herb garden, 91
bean leaf beetles, 127
beans, planting depth, 86
beds, vegetable garden, 83
beets, 24, 87
'Bell Boy,' sweet pepper, 88
beneficial insects, 138–139
Bermuda grass *(Cynodon dactylon)*,
    flaming, 156
'Big Rainbow,' tomato variety, 88
bindweed *(Convolvulus arvensis)*,
    digging/flaming, 155–156
bins, compost, 118–120
birds, fruit garden deterrents, 98
birdscare flash tape, 98
black plastic, unwanted growth
    removal, 45
black spot, 146–147
black vine weevils, 127
blackberries, fruit gardens, 97
'Blue Lake,' green bean variety, 88
blueberries, 51, 96
bordeaux mixture, fungicide, 150
borers, 127–128

botanical insecticides, 138
botanical names, 11–12
botrytis blight, 147
boxwood, winter injury, 26
bramble fruits, fruit gardens, 97
'Brandywine,' tomato variety, 88
broccoli, interplanting, 84
brown rot, 147
brush, garden site removal, 43–44
Bt *(Bacillus thuringiensis),* 138–140
burlap screens, winter injury, 26
'Buttercrunch,' lettuce variety, 88
bypass pruners, 30

• C •

cabbage, row arrangements, 83
calendars, vegetable gardens, 82
calendula, mild-winter regions, 24
caliche layer, metal-rod testing, 51
'California Wonder,' sweet
    pepper, 88
Capsella bursapastoris (shepherd's
    purse), seed pod removal, 158
carrots
  bed arrangements, 83
  planting depth, 87
  raised bed candidate, 61–62
  varieties, 88
carts, garden, 33
caterpillarss, 128
'Celebrity,' tomato variety, 88
celosia, spacing guidelines, 65
'Chantenay,' carrot variety, 88
chelated micronutrients, 112
Chenopodium album (lamb's-
    quarters), herbicides, 157
cherries, 94, 97
'Cherry Belle,' radish variety, 88
chickweed *(Stellaria media),* 156
children's play area, 9
chinch bugs, 128
Chinese praying mantis, 139
chipper-shredders, 38, 41
chives, herb garden, 91

clays, 47–48, 102
climate zones
  AHS Plant Heat-Zone Map, 16–18
  fruit gardens, 92–93
  growing season length, 13
  hardiness factors, 14–15
  microclimates, 6–7
  plant growth factor, 6–7
  USDA, 15–16, 19
  vegetable planning element, 81
  water needs factor, 102
  western North America, 17
clovers, 58
codling moths, 128–129
cold frames, plant starting, 20–21
coleus, spacing guidelines, 65
Colorado potato beetles, 129
common names, plants, 12
common thyme *(Thymus
    vulgaris),* 92
complete fertilizers, 111
compost starter, 121
composted manure, 55
composts
  anaerobic containers, 120
  bin types, 118–120
  hot compost containers, 119–120
  organic fertilizer, 115
  organic materials, 122
  pile building, 116–117
  soil amendment, 54–55
  static pile bins, 120
  teas, 123
  tools, 121–122
  tumblers, 120
conservation, water use, 108–109
container-grown trees and shrubs,
    69–73
containers
  anaerobic, 120
  hot compost, 119–120
  seedling purchase element, 64
  seedling removal, 66–67
  slow-release fertilizers, 113
  vegetable gardens, 83

'Contender' green bean variety, 88
Convolvulus arvensis (bindweed), 155–156
cool-season plants, starting, 20
copper, fungicide uses, 150
corn, 80, 83, 86
corn earworms, 129
corn gluten, nontoxic herbicide, 155
Corona's CLP Shear Maintenance Oil, 32
cotoneaster, multiseason shrub, 77
cover crops, nutrients, 57–58
covers, 23, 137, 154
cowpeas, 58
crabgrass *(Digitaria)*, 156–157
cross-pollination, fruit gardens, 94
cucumber beetles, 129–130
cucumbers, 83, 88
cultivars, naming conventions, 12
cultivation
   repeat, 46
   weed control technique, 154
cultivators/lightweight tillers, 38–41
curculios, 130
curly dock *(Rumex crispus)*, 157
cutworms, 130
Cynodon dactylon (Bermuda grass), flaming, 156
cytospora canker, 147

• D •

damping-off, 147
dandelion *(Taraxacum officinale)*, 157
'Dayton,' apple variety, 96
deep-rooted plants, 61–62
'Deer Tongue,' lettuce variety, 88
deer, wildlife controls, 151
design elements, 159–164
diatomaceous earth (DE), 140–141

Digitaria (crabgrass), 156–157
direct-sown seeds, 85–86
diseases, 104, 145–150
double digging, soil, 60–61
downy mildew, 148
drainage, percolation rate, 50–51
drifts, plant spacing technique, 65
drip irrigation, 105–106, 108
Dustin-Mizer, DE (diatomaceous earth) dispenser, 141

• E •

eastern exposures, 7, 25
eggplants, short-season, 24
electric bulb-planting drill, 41
electric rotary mowers, 36
electric string trimmers, 38
emitters, drip irrigation, 105–106
'Enchantment.' tomato variety, 88
'Enterprise,' apple variety, 96
entertainment space, gardening, 9
euonymus shrub, 26–27, 77
evaporation, plant water loss, 107
evapotranspiration, water loss, 107
evergreens, winter injury, 26

• F •

fake predators, bird deterrent, 98
'Fanfare,' cucumber variety, 88
fertilizers, 68, 110–115
firethorn, multiseason shrub, 77
flaming, weed control, 155–156
flea beetles, 131
floating row covers, 21–22, 137
flowering fruit shrub, 77
foliar fertilizers, hot weather, 112
food source, gardening reason, 9
'Freedom,' apple variety, 96
front tine tillers, 39
frost, 21–23, 81
frost-free days. *See* growing season
frost-tender plants, 20

fruit gardens
  bird deterrents, 98
  climate zones, 92–93
  climate/plant matching, 93
  cross-pollination, 94
  fertilizers, 94
  full sun, 94
  patience required, 93
  plant varieties, 95–99
  pollinizers, 94
  pruning, 95
  site planning, 94
  space requirements, 92–93
  thinning, 95
  water requirements, 94
  wind breaks, 94
fungicides, disease remedies, 150
furrow irrigation, water, 104–105
fusarium wilt, 150

• G •

garden carts, 33
garden hose, 30
garden sites
  design elements, 159–164
  reasons for, 9–10
  sod removal, 44–45
  soil preparations, 43–46
  solarization, 45–46
  unwanted growth removal, 43–46
garden supplies, sources, 42
garden tractors, 37
garlic, herb garden, 91
gasoline-powered trimmers, 38
genetics, water needs factor, 103
genus, naming conventions, 11
girding condition, 26–27
gloves, gardening, 33
'Gold Rush,' apple variety, 96
gophers, wildlife controls, 151
granular fertilizers, 112
grapes, fruit gardens, 97
grasses, sod stripping, 44–45

green beans, varieties, 88
green lacewing, 138
green manure crops, 57–58
grinders, 38, 41
groundhogs, wildlife controls, 152
growing seasons
  extending, 19–24
  frost-free days, 18–19
  plant growth factor, 18–19
  vegetable garden, 79–80
gypsy moths, 131
'Gypsy,' sweet pepper variety, 88

• H •

hand tools, 29–34
hand trowel, 30
hand watering, 103
handheld tiller/cultivator, 38–41
hardiness
  climate zone maps, 15–18
  plant growth factor, 14–15
  winter injury prevention, 25–27
hardpan, metal-rod testing, 51
hawthorn, animal damage, 26–27
heavenly bamboo, multiseason, 77
heaving, mulch prevention, 25
heirloom, vegetables, 89–90
herb gardens, plant varieties,
      90–92
herbicides, weed controls, 155
hills, vegetable garden, 83
hoes, 30–154
holly, 26, 77
home flower shop, 9
horticultural oils, use, 141–142
hose-end attachments, water, 103
hose-end sprinklers, 103–104
hoses, 30
hot beds, early plant starting, 21
hot caps, frost guards, 21
hot compost containers, 119–120
household junk, frost guard, 22–23
humus, 49–50, 55

hybrid vigor, vegetables, 89–90
hybrids, vegetable varieties, 89–90
hydrangea, multiseason shrub, 77

• I •

'Ichiban' Japanese eggplant, 24
inoculants, compost starter, 121
insecticidal soaps, 138, 142
insecticides, 138–145
insects, 126–138. *See also
individual type*
integrated pest management (IPM),
137–138
interplanting, vegetables, 84
irrigation systems, 104–106
IRT mulching film, soil heating, 23

• J •

Japanese beetles, 131–134
Japanese plums, 94
jar method, soil texture, 48–49
'Jonafree,' apple variety, 96
juniper, winter injury, 26

• K •

'Kentucky Wonder,' green bean
variety, 88

• L •

labels, 18, 84, 111
lady beetles, beneficial insect, 138
lamb's-quarters (*Chenopodium
album*), herbicides, 157
landscape fabrics, 154
lawn mowers, 34–37
lawn rakes, 30–31
lawn-and-garden tractors, 37
lawns, sod stripping, 44–45
leaf miners, 133
leafy greens, sunlight, 81

leggy condition, sunlight, 7
legumes, nutrients, 57–58
lemon thyme *(Thymus citriodorus)*,
herb garden, 92
'Lemon,' cucumber variety, 88
lettuce
bed arrangements, 83
cool-season vegetable, 80
interplanting, 84
mild-winter regions, 24
planting depth, 87
sunlight requirements, 81
varieties, 88
'Liberty,' apple variety, 96
lightweight tiller/cultivators, 38–41
lime sulfur, fungicide uses, 150
limestone, pH increase, 56–57
liquid fertilizers, 113
loams, ideal soil texture, 47–48
lobelia, spacing guidelines, 65
local extension office, 52, 94
lopping shears, 33–34
lubricants, hand tools, 32
lygus bugs (tarnished plant bugs),
136

• M •

'Macfree,' apple variety, 96
macronutrients, fertilizer, 110
mail-order, garden tools, 41–42
maintenance tasks, hand tools, 32
manures, 55, 115
marjoram, *(Origanum majorana)*
herb garden, 91
'McShay,' apple variety, 96
mealybugs, 133
melons, 24, 83
Mentha piperita (peppermint), 91
metal-rod method, soil, 50–51
Mexican bean beetles, 133
microclimates, plant growth, 6–7
micronutrients, fertilizer, 110–111
mildews, 148
mild-winter regions, 24

mini-tillers, 39–41
mints, herb garden, 91
moisture loss, winter injury, 26
moisture testing, 106–108
mold, overhead watering, 104
mother-of-thyme *(Thymus praecox arcticus)*, herb garden, 92
mountain ash, 26–27
mulch
  clear plastic, 23
  IRT mulching film, 23
  seedlings, 68
  vegetable garden weed control, 87
  water conservation, 108
  weed control technique, 154
  winter injury prevention, 25–26
mulching rotary mowers, 36

• *N* •

'Nantes,' carrot variety, 88
native plants, benefits, 8
neem, 138, 142–143
'Nevada,' lettuce variety, 88
newspapers, site-clearing, 46
noisemakers, bird deterrent, 98
nonlegumes, nutrients, 57–58
nontoxic herbicides, 155
North America, USDA hardiness zone map, 15–16
northern exposures, 7, 25
'Nova Easygro,' apple variety, 96
'Novamac,' apple variety, 96
nurseries, 42, 64, 69, 74–76
nutrients
  fertilizer components, 110–111
  soil adjustments, 57–58

• *O* •

observation, water needs, 108
onions, seeds versus bulbs, 88
open pollinated, vegetables, 90
oregano *(Origanum vulgare)*, 91
'Oregon Trail,' pea variety, 88

organic fertilizers, 113, 115
organic matter
  compost piles, 122
  soil amendments, 53–56
  soil structure enhancement, 49–50
oriental fruit moths, 133
Origanum majorana (marjoram), 91
Origanum vulgare (oregano), 91
oscillating hoes, 30
overhead watering, 104
oxalis, herbicides, 157

• *P* •

painted daisy *(Tanacetum cineraiifolium)*, 143–144
pansies, mild-winter regions, 24
parasitic nematodes, 138
parsley, herb garden, 91–92
parsnips, raised bed, 61–62
peach leaf curl, 148–149
peaches, fruit gardens, 92–93, 97
pears, 94, 98
peas, 80, 84, 88
peat moss, soil amendment, 56
peppermint *(Mentha piperita)*, 91
peppers, 24, 80, 81
percolation rate, drainage, 50–51
perennials, winter injury, 25
pesticides. *See* insecticides
pests, 98, 137–138, 151–152
pets, gardening reason, 9
pH factors, 51–52, 56–57, 94
pheromones (synthetic), 129
photinia, multiseason shrub, 77
photosynthesis, plant feeding, 109
phytophthora blight, 149
pinching off, seedlings, 64
pitchforks, compost piles, 122
plants
  botanical naming, 11–12
  days to harvest information, 18
  fertilizer suggestions, 114–115
  frost guards, 21–23
  girding prevention, 26–27

growing seasons, 18–19
growth factors, 6–8
hardiness factors, 14–15
native, 8
photosynthesis, 109
starting indoors, 20
plastic collars, girding, 27
plastic covers, site-clearing, 45–46
plastic film, mulch, 23
plow pan, overtilling concern, 60
plums, 94, 98
pollinizers, fruit garden, 94
polyester bird netting, 98
Portulaca oleracea (purslane), 158
potatoes, row arrangements, 83
powdery mildew, 148
power cultivators, 38–41
power tools
  grinders, 38, 41
  lawn mowers, 34–37
  purchasing guidelines, 34–41
  string trimmers, 37–38
  tillers, 38–41
power-reel mowers, 35
pressure pan, overtilling, 60
'Prima,' apple variety, 96
primary nutrients, 110–111
primrose, mild-winter regions, 24
'Priscilla,' apple variety, 96
'Pristine,' apple variety, 96
private getaway, gardening, 9
prostrate spurge, herbicides, 158
pruners, 30
pruning, fruit gardens, 95
pumpkins, sunlight, 81
purslane *(Portulaca oleracea),* 158
push rotary power mowers, 35–36
push-reel mowers, 35
pyrethrins, use guidelines, 143–144

● *R* ●

radishes, 80, 83 88
rain gauge, water conservation,
  109

rainfall, soil pH factors, 51
rainwater, water conservation, 109
raised beds, 61–62, 84–85
rakes, 30–31
raspberries, fruit gardens, 97
rear tine tillers, 39
'Redfree,' apple variety, 96
redroot pigweed *(Amaranthus
  retroflexus),* herbicides, 158
relaxation, gardening reason, 10
remedy fungicide, 150
repeat cultivation, 46
Rhizobium, nitrogen-fixing, 58
Rhododendron, 26, 51
ribbons-and-bows, soil texture, 48
riding mowers, 36
rock gardens, winter injury, 25
rodent repellents, girding, 27
root flare, balled-and-burlapped
  plants, 76
root maggots, 134
roots
  garden site removal, 43–44
  heaving prevention, 25
  inspecting when purchasing, 64
  root flare, 76
'Rosa Bianca' eggplant, 24
rosemary, herb garden, 92
roses, 61–62, 77
rotenone, 138, 144
row covers, frost guard, 21–22
rows, vegetable garden, 83
Rumex crispus (curly dock), 157
rusts, 149

● *S* ●

sage *(Salvia officinalis),* 92
sands, 47–48, 102
scab, apple disease problem, 96
scales, 134
'Scallopini,' summer squash, 88
scarecrows, bird deterrent, 98
'Scarlet Globe,' radish variety, 88
scuffle hoes, 30

second crops, growing season, 23
secondary nutrients, fertilizer, 110
seed tapes, vegetable gardens, 87
seedlings, 64–68, 85–86. *See also*
    transplants
seeds, 85–87
self-propelled rotary mowers, 36
shade conditions, growth factor, 7
shade exposures, water needs, 102
shallow-rooted plants, 25
shepherd's purse *(Capsella*
    bursapastoris), 158
'Short n' Sweet,' carrot variety, 88
shovels, 30–31, 58–60
shrubs, 69–73
sifter, compost piles, 121–122
silts, soil texture type, 47–48
single digging, soil, 58–59
'Sir Prize,' apple variety, 96
slow-release fertilizers, 113
snails/slugs, 134–135
sod, stripping techniques, 44–45
soil mixes
    acidity, 51–52
    alkalinity, 51–52
    amendments, 52–58
    caliche layer, 51
    double digging, 60–61
    green manure crops, 57–58
    hardpan, 51
    jar testing method, 48–49
    local extension office testing, 52
    loosening techniques, 58–61
    metal-rod testing, 50–51
    nutrient adjustments, 57–58
    percolation rate testing, 50–51
    pH factors, 51–52
    plant growth factor, 8
    raised beds, 61–62
    ribbons-and-bows test
        method, 48
    single digging, 58–60
    structure, 49–51
    textures, 47–49
    vegetable garden, 84–85
    water needs factor, 102
    working condition evaluations, 59

solarization, 23, 45–46, 145–146,
    154
sooty mold, 150
sources, garden tools, 41–42
southern exposures, full sun, 7
soybeans, 58
spacing, 65, 84, 93
species, naming conventions, 11
spider mites, 135–136
spinach, 81–87
spirea, multiseason shrub, 77
spotted spurge, herbicides, 158
spreaders, granular fertilizers, 112
sprinklers, 23, 103–104
Spritzer tube duster, 141
squash, 81, 83, 86, 88
stakes, trees/shrubs, 72–73
static pile compost bins, 120
steel-bow rakes, 31
Stellaria media (chickweed), 156
stiff-tined rakes, 31
stock, mild-winter regions, 24
strawberries, 25, 99
string trimmers, 37–38
structure, soil combinations, 49–51
succession planting, vegetables, 84
'Sugar Snap,' pea variety, 88
sulfur, 56–57, 150
summer squash, varieties, 88
sun exposures, water needs, 102
'Sunburst,' summer squash, 88
sunlight, 7, 81–82, 109
'Super Sugar Mel,' pea variety, 88
sweet alyssum, spacing, 65
'Sweet Banana,' sweet pepper, 88
sweet cherries, 94, 97
sweet peppers, varieties, 88
'Sweet Success,' cucumber, 88

• *T* •

tamping down, seedlings, 67–68
Tanacetum cineraiifolium (painted
    daisy), pyrethrins, 143–144
tape measure, 33

Taraxacum officinale (dandelion), 157
tarnished plant bugs (lygus bugs), 136
teas, compost, 123
temperatures
 AHS Plant Heat-Zone Map, 16–18
 USDA hardiness zone map, 15–16
 vegetable garden planning, 81
tent caterpillars, 136
textures, soil types, 47–49
thermometers, compost piles, 121
thinning, fruit gardens, 95
thyme, herb garden, 92
Thymus citriodorus (lemon thyme), 92
Thymus praecox arcticus (mother-of-thyme), 92
Thymus vulgaris (common thyme), 92
tillers
 plow pan condition, 60
 pressure pan condition, 60
 purchasing guidelines, 38–41
 repeat cultivation, 46
 single digging technique, 58–60
timers, 104–106, 108
tobira, multiseason shrub, 77
tomato hornworms, 136–137
tomatoes, 24, 80–81, 83, 88–89
tools, 29–42, 121, 122
topsoils, soil amendment, 55–56
'Touchon,'172 carrot variety, 88
transpiration, plant water loss, 107
transplants, 20, 70–77. *See also* seedlings
traps, 134–135, 138
trees
 fruit gardens, 92–99
 girding prevention, 26–27
 healthy plant indicators, 69
 planting process, 70–73
 staking at planting, 72–73
trichogramma wasps, 138
trimmers (string), 37–38
trowels, 30

tumblers, compost bin, 120
turnips, 83–87
twine, winter injury prevention, 26

• U •

U.S. Customs, imported plants, 132
U.S. Department of Agriculture (USDA), 15–16, 19

• V •

varieties, naming conventions, 11
vegetable gardens, 79–87
 beds, 83
 climate zones, 81
 containers, 83
 direct-sown seeds, 85–86
 frost-resistant crops, 85–86
 frost-tender crops, 86
 growing season limitations, 79–80
 harvesting guidelines, 87
 heirloom varieties, 89–90
 herbs, 90–92
 hills, 83
 hybrid varieties, 89–90
 hybrid vigor, 89–90
 interplanting, 84
 mulch for weed control, 87
 open pollinated varieties, 90
 pH balance guidelines, 84
 planting arrangements, 83–84
 planting calendars, 82
 raised beds, 84–85
 rows, 83
 seed depth guidelines, 86–87
 seed tapes, 87
 seedlings, 85–86
 size guidelines, 82–83
 soil improvements, 84–85
 spacing considerations, 84
 succession planting, 84
 sunlight requirements, 81–82
 water at planting, 87
 weed removal, 87

venticillium wilt, 150
vetches, 58
viburnum, 26–27, 77

• W •

water
  at vegetable garden planting, 87
  automated systems, 106
  climate factors, 102
  conservation techniques, 108–109
  delivery systems, 103–106
  drip irrigation, 105–106
  evapotranspiration, 107
  fruit gardens, 94
  furrow irrigation, 104–105
  hand watering, 103
  overhead watering disease, 104
  plant growth factor, 8
  seedling guidelines, 68
  soil type factors, 102
  sprinklers, 103–104
  sun/shade factors, 102
  volume needs, 106–108
  weather factors, 102
water wands, 33
water-filled cloche, frost guard, 21
weather, water needs factor, 102
Web sites
  A.M. Leonard, Inc., 29
  AHS Heat-Zone Map, 18
  APHIS (Animal and Plant Health
    Inspection Service), 132
  Corona's CLP Shear Maintenance
    Oil, 32
  Park Seed Co., 41
  Perma-Guard, Inc., 141
  Sunset zone maps, 17
  U.S. Customs regulations, 132
  USDA hardiness zone map, 15

weed eraser, herbicide, 155
weeds. *See also individual weeds*
  control techniques, 153–154
  flaming, 155–156
  garden site removal, 43–44
  nontoxic herbicides, 155
  oxalis, 157
  prostrate spurge, 158
  spotted spurge, 158
  vegetable gardens, 87
  water conservation, 109
western exposures, 7
western North America, zone
    maps, 17
'White Icicle,' radish variety, 88
whiteflies, 137
wildlife, 26–27, 98, 151–152
'Williams' Pride,' apple variety, 96
wilts, 150
wind breaks, fruit gardens, 94
winter gardening, benefits, 24
winter injury, prevention, 25–27
wire composter, 118
woodchucks, wildlife controls, 152
wooden compost bin, 119
work area, gardening reason, 9–10

• Y •

year-round-gardening, benefits, 24
'Yellow Crookneck,' summer
    squash variety, 88
yew, winter injury prevention, 26

• Z •

zigzag patterns, plant spacing, 65
zones, USDA (U.S. Department of
    Agriculture) maps, 15–16

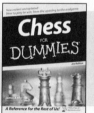

SPORTS, FITNESS, PARENTING, RELIGION & SPIRITUALITY

0-471-76871-5   0-7645-7841-3

Also available:

- Catholicism For Dummies
0-7645-5391-7
- Exercise Balls For Dummies
0-7645-5623-1
- Fitness For Dummies
0-7645-7851-0
- Football For Dummies
0-7645-3936-1
- Judaism For Dummies
0-7645-5299-6
- Potty Training For Dummies
0-7645-5417-4
- Buddhism For Dummies
0-7645-5359-3

- Pregnancy For Dummies
0-7645-4483-7 †
- Ten Minute Tone-Ups
For Dummies
0-7645-7207-5
- NASCAR For Dummies
0-7645-7681-X
- Religion For Dummies
0-7645-5264-3
- Soccer For Dummies
0-7645-5229-5
- Women in the Bible
For Dummies
0-7645-8475-8

TRAVEL

0-7645-7749-2   0-7645-6945-7

Also available:

- Alaska For Dummies
0-7645-7746-8
- Cruise Vacations For Dummies
0-7645-6941-4
- England For Dummies
0-7645-4276-1
- Europe For Dummies
0-7645-7529-5
- Germany For Dummies
0-7645-7823-5
- Hawaii For Dummies
0-7645-7402-7

- Italy For Dummies
0-7645-7386-1
- Las Vegas For Dummies
0-7645-7382-9
- London For Dummies
0-7645-4277-X
- Paris For Dummies
0-7645-7630-5
- RV Vacations For Dummies
0-7645-4442-X
- Walt Disney World & Orlando
For Dummies
0-7645-9660-8

GRAPHICS, DESIGN & WEB DEVELOPMENT

0-7645-8815-X   0-7645-9571-7

Also available:

- 3D Game Animation For
Dummies
0-7645-8789-7
- AutoCAD 2006 For Dummies
0-7645-8925-3
- Building a Web Site For
Dummies
0-7645-7144-3
- Creating Web Pages All-in-
One Desk Reference For
Dummies
0-7645-4345-8
- Dreamweaver 8 For Dummies
0-7645-9649-7
- InDesign CS2 For Dummies
0-7645-9572-5

- Macromedia Flash 8
For Dummies
0-7645-9691-8
- Photoshop CS2 and Digital
Photography For Dummies
0-7645-9580-6
- Photoshop Elements 4
For Dummies
0-471-77483-9
- Syndicating Web Sites with
RSS Feeds For Dummies
0-7645-8848-6
- Yahoo! SiteBuilder
For Dummies
0-7645-9800-7

NETWORKING, SECURITY, PROGRAMMING & DATABASES

0-7645-7728-X   0-471-74940-0

Also available:

- Access 2003 All-in-One Desk
Reference For Dummies
0-7645-3988-4
- ASP.NET 2 For Dummies
0-7645-7907-X
- C# 2005 For Dummies
0-7645-9704-3
- Excel VBA Programming
For Dummies
0-7645-7412-4
- Hacking For Dummies
0-7645-5784-X
- Hacking Wireless Networks
For Dummies
0-7645-9730-2

- Microsoft SQL Server 2005
For Dummies
0-7645-7755-7
- Networking All-in-One Desk
Reference For Dummies
0-7645-9939-9
- Preventing Identity Theft
For Dummies
0-7645-7336-5
- Telecom For Dummies
0-471-77085-X
- Visual Studio 2005 All-in-One
Desk Reference For Dummies
0-7645-9775-2
- XML For Dummies
0-7645-8845-1

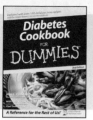

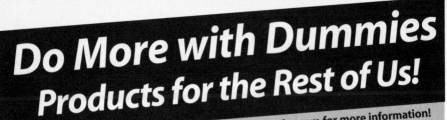

Portable Gardening Guides

**Each book includes
8 pages of full-color
garden photos!**

Notes